The Accelerated (2013)

The Dear Queen Journey (2014)

Dear Soul: Love after Pain (2014)

Dear Love Life (2015)

This Is What Real Love Feels Like (2016)

Lust for Life (2017)

Care Package: A Path to Deep Healing (2018)

Free Your Energy (2019)

Loving Yourself Properly (2021)

Loving Yourself Properly

SYLVESTER MCNUTT III

ISBN-13: 978-0-578-60328-5

The names in all these stories, poems, and anecdotes have been changed to protect the identities of any person(s), real, exaggerated, or made up. *Loving Yourself Properly* and Sylvester McNutt III are not suggesting or promoting any lifestyle or choices in this book. This book is written as a true expression of art, poetry, and creativity. This book is written from the perspective and opinion of the creator, and he reserves the right, at any moment, to change his perception of anything presented. The author, the publisher, or the person responsible for delivering you this text is not liable for any undesirable outcome.

All social media links, contact info, bio, and speaking dates can be found at www.sylvestermcnutt.net

10 9 8 7 6 5 4 3 2 1

Contents

Introduction

This is a friendly invitation into your darkness, into your light, into your wholeness. Self-love is always about wholeness.

LOVING YOURSELF PROPERLY MEANS LOVING YOURSELF FULLY.

Yes, that means even the parts that sit in the shadows of who you pretend to show the world, even the parts that we may not want to show. Safely, my friend, we have to visit our shadows and darkness, because that is the only way to get the full image, the full picture and that is where love resides — in fullness.

You are about to read a bold claim, tell me if you believe this: your belief system and your thoughts lead to your choices, and your choices lead to your habits, and your habits lead to your outcomes and your emotional experience.

I want to see and have the ability to access the emotional experiences that give me inspiration, peace of mind, and harmony — don't you? I want to feel growth, love and like what I do matters — don't you? If so, then we have to accept and honor all of the sides of us. **Total acceptance is the direct path to genuine self-love.**

This journey is about us making space for the

outcast parts of our soul that we hide, for the parts of our personality that we are too afraid to show. Why? So you can add new stitches into your wounds, so you can add new mindsets and begin to untangle old ones, and so you can begin to recognize and present yourself fully which will lead to richer relationships, deeper meaning, and more clarity.

This invitation is about finding your voice—the voice of passion and fire, if you so dare to allow it to be ignited. The invitation here is going to ask you to sit still and acknowledge what you see, and it also will make space for you to spring into action to create what you think is possible.

The invitation here isn't about being better, gaining more, or making improvement—this invitation is about beginning to deeply introspect our choices, emotions and habits. This invitation wants you to see the darkness and the light, and it serves as an opportunity to let go of beliefs and behaviors that keep you out of your highest alignment. Life is not hard or easy, it is a puzzle and this invitation is about finding pieces, and moving them around to make an image.

This invitation is not about shame, putting yourself down or chasing perfection in fact — this invitation is asking you to acknowledge all three and then begin to choose new plays out of your playbook of life. *Loving Yourself Properly* is a playbook, an invitation to call an audible on how we are treating, seeing and talking about our journey.

***

I always hear people say things like "Just love yourself" or "Hey, let it go" or "Just get over it." And although those phrases are important, I've always felt like they are missing something, they are missing the magic needed to move the needle on what's happening in our experience.

For about a week straight, I heard people saying, "Just love yourself." And in my head, one day I said, *How do people know how to love themselves properly if all they talk about in school is social studies and a watered-down, untruthful history?* And it was through that conscious thought that the title *Loving Yourself Properly* came to me.

It took me about a week to spring into action as far as writing the book was concerned. You'll learn in the opening paragraphs about a conversation that triggered the action when I already had the thought brewing. For context, I started writing this right upon finishing my book *Free Your Energy* circa summer 2018. It took me a full two years to write, which is my longest interval between books. Life brought me some changes and some challenges. I had a kid, the world had a pandemic, and I felt called to get in the best shape of my life mentally, physically, and spiritually. All that happening in a two-year period caused a lot of learning, a lot of letting go and realignment.

I feel convinced that the poetry, stories, ideas, and words you'll see here can support you in your journey. If I can get through that two-year period and come out on the other end with the high vibrational feeling that I have now, let me just say I am excited for you.

I believe the purpose of this book is to support you, to ask you questions, and to act as a call to action. I genuinely hope that the invitation that this book is feels warm but direct. I am not the type of writer who wants to write fluff to appease a readership. My mission is to cause a disruption in how you currently think about your life and I hope that disruption gives you the permission to create a new paradigm for how your reality will unfold. If you come across anything that is offensive, I'm sorry; however, keep reading, ha! It's okay, get uncomfortable and get in the unfamiliar.

Last, don't read this book and say "I agree" or "I disagree." This book isn't here to seek agreement or approval; it's best used as a tool to reflect, to hold space for your own thought, and to dive deeper into your psyche. If I was reading this book, I would create a men's or women's group to meet once a week and discuss each chapter. Note that I'm in a men's group now, and we meet and discuss books, current events, what is going on in our lives, and other topics that seem potent to us at the time. Of course, you could read this book on your own, which I know will offer you a depth and intimacy that you've been craving.

From a structural standpoint I believe that a deconstruction of our belief system followed by a conscious reconstruction phase makes the most sense and that is how I aimed to write this book.

In *Loving Yourself Properly*, we start off by diving into our shame wounds (deconstruction). My theory is that on the other side of shame is where we unlock the deepest connection to ourselves. Shame blocks us and keeps us out of connection with the world and ourselves. I have started the book off there because it's a topic that nobody wants to talk about, so I have felt it incumbent on me to create a safe space for that conversation early—don't be sacred and keep reading because we need to peel the layers of your shame.

The first three chapters feel like a missile landing into your belief systems — a true deconstruction, if you will, as we tear down your identity, your walls, your thoughts, your habits. And then the rest of the book feels restorative, healing, and full of love and compassion. I feel like, together, this is a complete body of work that can truly be used for the greater good of the collective consciousness.

As a self-published author, it is an honor to be able to bring you my ninth book, *Loving Yourself Properly*. I do not take you, your time, or your effort to obtain this book for granted.

You'll see poems, points of reflection, affirmations, or short ideas in the chapters as well. I do that for two reasons: one, to pull out particular points to focus on, and because I grew up as a poetry writer so I love trying to find the simple complexities in language, and allowing those to stand alone. Second, I love having pages with short-to-the-point words accompanied by longer and complete thoughts. I find it to be aesthetic, easy to read, and easy to refer back to later. My current readers already know this about my writing style and now you do too! I'm sending you all the love, and I hope great things happen for you once you finish reading *Loving Yourself Properly*.

Warmly,

Sylvester McNutt III

Affirmation On New Beginnings:

I am open to change, to love, to new habits, and to a new reality. I am open to new beginnings and what they offer to my community and me. I recognize that I am enough as I am, today. I realize that I am a loving being who makes a difference in the lives of others. I am embracing the potential inside me, and I am grateful for everything that I currently have. I release everything that is less than love.

— Sylvester McNutt III

1

Summer's story: shame-based Thinking

IT WAS A WARM LATE-SUMMER EVENING HERE IN PHOENIX, ARIZONA.

I lay on the gray couch, looking up at the black ceiling fan as the wind landed on my soul from the oscillation. The heat here was dry but inspiring, and there was little to no humidity floating around in the air, but it was so hot that you can feel the warmth dancing in the air with every inhale and exhale. There was an unusual breeze that swept through my three-story loft as I listened intently to my dear friend Summer on the phone. The breeze felt green, like a pasture. It felt purple, like when the sun is setting and the refractions of light bank off of the rocks and buildings.

Among the two ceiling fans, the central air, and the oscillating fan that sat adjacent to my TV stand, there was a calming white noise that pulsated through the living quarters. As the mum sound of the air-conditioning circled around me, I fell into the enchanted spell of the present moment. I understood there was more to her words than what she was saying. I could hear the inner motivations and what was making her move as she expressed what was on her mind.

I heard her say, "Ugh, Sly, I'm just not good enough for a healthy relationship. I always found myself in the same mess." She fumed and dumped emotional garbage on herself. She spewed self-defeating thoughts and limiting beliefs through the airwaves like a 1990's pop song on TRL. I could feel the anger, doubt, fear, and vulnerability capture every thought that escaped her essence. With each moment` she tumbled into the depths of introspection; the wave of her tone bounced through my ear as I observed the conversation. Her frustration, to me was a good thing, she was listening to her soul as it was saying, "This current version of your life is not your full expression, it's not your highest reality — please, get us there."

"I hear you" was the most I said for a few moments, and then I said it again. "I hear you, Summer. I totally get where you are coming from." The space between the times when I spoke was grand, but it was enough for her to know she was safe and heard. Summer was melting away layers of wax that had accumulated over the year, she finally was cooking the material of her life.

We talked on the phone for an hour or so, me offering my ear while she offered her narratives. She complained about what he wasn't doing well, who he was not, and why nothing was going right in their relationship. Her gripes soon turned into tears of sorrow and hopelessness, a release that she needed. I knew that this moment was about listening and not about direction, and also, I could feel goose bumps grow on my forearms as ideas started crawling into my brain. I offered no advice, only a safe space to share, which was what she needed.

I went from lying to sitting up on my gray couch, wearing black shorts and a fresh haircut, not judging but listening, diving deeply into every complaint, asking questions about why and how. I never offered my advice or opinion but just listened to her until I gathered enough data from her transmission. This was someone who had offered me her ear when I had been in places of confusion and introspection. We had a relationship with a deep connection that was fueled through laughter, fitness, positive memories, and conversations like these. She felt I offered a safe space where she could vent and share her ideas. And although I was just listening to her at the time, I could feel my inspiration moving toward this conversation in the same way that my earlier books *Care Package* and *Free Your Energy* were sparked.

When it was finally my turn to respond to everything that she unloaded, I said, "First, I have to say thank you for sharing, and I hope you felt safe. You have just ignited something in me, something that was brewing for a few years. You know, listening to you talk about this is making me want to write a book. It's making me want to ask a thousand questions. I feel like so many of us could benefit from going on a journey of self-love, a journey where we unlock another layer of love through stories and words, the ideas that can free us, ideas that we can bring back to our community, to our family, to strangers who come across us, to ourselves."

She laughed at first. I could hear her smile coming through the phone as she said, "I'm honored. I think you should write a book about self-love, and you should also give me the first copy."

We both laughed, and then I said, "Ha! Damn, girl,

everyone always wants something for free these days — that's is what is wrong with our generation, ha, jeez."

"If you're serious about writing it, what would it be about?" she inquired.

"It would be about loving yourself properly and figuring out how to invite yourself into your highest connection, into your highest vibration. Essentially, the problems you are talking about have nothing to do with this guy or the relationship you have with him. The problems you have are actually internal. Your problems have gone from relationship to relationship. I think you have a relationship with yourself that needs some care. You have self-love problems, you have a problem with boundaries, you have an issue with how you're treating yourself. It sounds like you have wounds that need attention. And the relationships in your life are trying to show you that you need to look within, do some inner healing and create a vision for how you want your life to be. Because I know you, I know a lot of the problems you are facing are rooted in wounds. You need to go on a journey of figuring out how to love yourself properly, to be honest," I said in a calm tone with a smooth rhythm.

I went to my kitchen to grab my notebook. My black forty-ounce thermos of water sat right next to my notebook. I took a sip of water, which was a little under room temperature, and I grabbed the white journal. The binding on the journal was shabby and weak. I can tell that a new journal was looming on the horizon because my withered old faithful was becoming thin and full of content, poems and words, full of ideas.

"Wow. Thank you. You always know what to say. Damn, I need to work on myself—you're right. So, um, Sly, what is the first step of loving yourself properly?"

"Ha! I think I am going to go now," I said with a smirk from ear to ear.

"Wait, you're not going to answer my question, Sly. What is the first step of loving yourself properly?"

"I am going to answer your question. I am about to cancel my plans, stretch, and figure out how to express my thoughts on that question. But you know, I want to thank you. I want to thank you for showing up for yourself," I said with vigor and confidence. When we ended our phone call, I sat down on that same couch with a big smile on my face, a smile that took me into a cloud of thoughts, ideas, and possibilities.

I will always be grateful for Summer—without her voice, her expression, we wouldn't be here at this point together as students and friends. I will always be grateful for the summer as it heats up and cooks the ideas that we plant in the spring. I've grown to love the seasons; they teach us about change, grief, and beauty.

WHAT IS THE FIRST STEP TO SELF-LOVE?

Simply, the first step of self-love is **to come to the present moment and accept yourself as you are right now, and to not judge yourself, at all.** But Sylvester, "That is not possible for me because I am this, and I am that, and I do not have enough of this or that". False, with compassion, you are using shame-based thinking to limit your perception. Self-love is built by accepting yourself as you are right now. It's not about pleasure, it's not about more, it's not about getting better or improving. Self-love is allowing your body to surrender to your mind, it's choosing to be totally present, it's choosing to say this is me today and I am not enslaved, I am not trapped, I am not a victim, I love myself as I am right now.

For anything from *Loving Yourself Properly* to make sense, there are a few building blocks that are crucial to our practice. We have to bring into our awareness how we use shame-based thinking. Shame-based thinking is a consistent awareness of our defects or perceived shortcomings, a constant awareness that brings these alleged character flaws or defects into our waking consciousness. It's so widely repeated that, often, we aren't even aware of it when we do it to others.

When you ask most people to love themselves as they are right now their excuses will be laced with shame-based thinking. You'll hear people say things like, 'Well once I get my degree then I'll be lovable." And that's not true. You'll get the degree and because you didn't accept yourself before, you'll then crave more eduction, more certificates, or more external validation (creating the chase for destination addiction). **The first step to self-love is to accept yourself fully as you are right now**. There is a part of you, right now, that knows this fully — instinctually. If there is a piece of you that has you fighting these words, just know that is shame-based thinking.

Let's go deeper.

The two problems with shame-based thinking are that (1) it's common in our society, you can tell that simply by observing people's talk patterns and that (2) it can drastically prohibit us from adding self-love into our life. Shame-based thinking leads to speaking with shame, and as long as shame is at the forefront of our thoughts, actions, and perceptions, how can we invite love into that space? I've never been able to recognize and feel shame and love at the same time; have you? If you are like me and you've never had shame and love at the same time, then it looks like they may occupy similar spaces.

An example of shame-based thinking from Summer's story is when she alludes to being unworthy of healthy relationships. First, that kind of statement is false, but she's making that comment because of her frustration with the partnership that she has entered. She's saying a limiting belief which then subconsciously tells her mind to support and put energy behind that belief, and of course, her life will follow that limiting belief. Later, we talk about limiting beliefs but one of the biggest anchors of them is shame. Shame is the gear that grinds limiting beliefs.

The first step toward loving yourself properly is to allow yourself to be fully aware of shame-based thinking; in fact, it may be advantageous to your journey if you took notes throughout your reflections as you answer the questions posed by this book. Journaling as you read this book could bring you clarity, but it won't be because of the text or the author or anything outside of you. Your clarity will only come through your own experience, realization, and beliefs.

I notice that there's a recipe to identify a shame-based thought: ***I am + negative word or phrase*** that reflects actions, attitudes, standing in life, or behavior. If you take a few minutes to write down or to say aloud the shame-based phrases that you share to yourself, you might be alarmed to see what they sound like.

THROW AWAY THESE SELF-DEFEATING SHAME-BASED PHRASES:

- I'm terrible.
- I am broken.
- I am unloved.
- I don't matter.
- I am unwanted.
- I am unworthy of …..
- I am not good enough for …
- I am + any phrases that brings you down, keeps you small or prevents you from your fullest expression.

Actually, let's stop there; you get to the point—there's no reason to keep typing up more statements that don't lift your spirit. Even typing those out begins to drain my energy, this is why I don't use these phrases and I'm inviting you to let them go, as well. Reading them or saying them with this consciousness that you have now even makes those phrases feel off because now you recognize that they don't lift you—they don't offer you love.

The reason they feel that way is that they don't align with your soul; they don't align with the love you currently have inside you or the love you want to experience through connection with others. Those are words that bring a weight to your soul, a hindrance if you will (and trust, you are free to release them in this moment if you'd like).

Let's take the last shame-based example that I listed and expand it for the sake of understanding the depth of this practice. Take a look at this shame-based sentence: *I am broken, and nobody will ever care about me the way I care about them.* Think about the power of your consciousness when you intake shame-based sentences daily. I want you to ask yourself, What are you telling yourself each day as you live? Are you telling yourself phrases over and over like "I am broken"? *I am broken* is already a sentence that contains a lot of uninterpreted depth to it, and then adding in *nobody will ever care about me the way I care about them* does more damage to your journey than good because now it locks the future with a statement that isn't true. Can you see the harm in shame-based thinking now?

Our homework is to take an inventory of what our shame-based statements are and where they show up in our lives. They can show up in relationship with self, in career, in family, in the way we naturally talk about the world and ourselves. This practice is crucial to developing self-love, and if we can begin to get small victories with this, the rest of the journey can reveal itself to us faster.

I will argue that the potency of shame-based thinking can have many different variances as well, and it's important for us to delineate how some can affect us very little and how some instances may seem overwhelming. Regardless of how potent one instance may be versus another, if we think about it in terms of a bank account, we can learn a lot. Let's assume that every shame-based thought lasts for two minutes.

When Reggie presents his food to his new girlfriend, he often gives it with shame-based phrases. He says something like, "Here's your milkshake. *I didn't add enough* oat milk to it, and I didn't have any cinnamon. I hope it's okay."

Another time, he presents a salmon meal to her and says, "*I'm not the best* at cooking salmon; think it's a little dry, but here it is." Look at the italicized words in the sentences to see what is triggering the shame-based recipe we have cooked up earlier. The recipe is ***I am + negative word of phrase*** that reflects actions, attitudes, standing in life, or behavior.

Friend, why? Why do that? How does it sound? Are these examples huge deal breakers, and do they mean that the food is going to be awful? No way. It could be both the best salmon and the best milkshake of her life, so why is it not presented that way? In this situation, we are sharing food, and food is a gift—another way to show love is to offer food, to share food, to share intimacy through conversation and connection over a meal.

So instead, offer the milkshake like this: "I made a milkshake. It contains love and oat milk." Instead of mentioning what you're not good at, thank the person for the space to display yourself. Offer the salmon like this: "Thank you for allowing me to make you dinner. Thank you for sharing this space with me. Dinner is served, my lady.

Tonight's plate features salmon, broccoli, and Spanish rice. I took that salmon right out of the ocean this morning while you were asleep. Ha!"

When I think about offering the milkshake, the salmon, your thoughts, your love, your friendship, your ear, I think of it as an opportunity to connect. I think of it as an opportunity to invite someone into your space as a way to express yourself. I, too, have shame-based thoughts and phrases, and what I'm noticing is that the more I practice replacing them and being aware of them, the lighter I feel. I offer this to you as a practice, one that has aided me in feeling lighter and free.

Growing up in the West puts us into a constant state of competition and domination and, we are addicted to the win-loss mindset. And we've grown to look at our emotional expressions as a win or a loss, and to me, that takes away our humanity. It takes away our ability to love ourselves properly, to observe objectively and to judge ourselves without shame or guilt. There is a lot of peace that happens when we begin to identify, acknowledge, and work with those shame-based thoughts we come up with.

Fall in love with the way you use words.

Use your words wisely. Words act in the same way water does: they have the ability to nourish, heal and keep you alive. They also can destroy everything. Fall in love with how you use language.

--- Sylvester McNutt III

Affirmations To use daily

That build you up

- I am enough
- I am more than enough
- I have more than enough
- I am not lacking; I am well.
- I am willing to learn and grow.
- I am enough as I am, right now.
- I accept who I am without shame.
- I'm proud of what I've overcome so far.
- I'm so happy to know that there is enough for me.
- I'm so happy that opportunity always comes my way.
- When I want something, I will go for it, but not because I lack but because I am aligned.

What If You Feel Shame Once You Identify a Shame-Based Thought?

The answer is so much simpler than you think it may be. You may have a shame-based thought, and then you may feel more shame now that you're aware of it. I view this moment as a victory actually because, previously, you weren't aware of it, and now you are *(this is you recognizing a patterns, which means you have the power to shift your response)*. That shift in awareness is powerful; it allows us to process our observation one level deeper. And to me, that observation does not mean judging the emotion or observation; it means acknowledging that you are seeing your own emotional process right in front of you.

To be able to say, "I notice that I am encountering shame," is excellent, and now, how you respond after that observation is what you want to consider.

Instead of allowing shame to get you down, once you identify shame, offer yourself a moment of laughter or take a moment to hug yourself (a healing, self-soothing tactic). Or if someone is around, hug them and tell them about what you have become aware of.

Tell them about your victory and celebrate that joy with them. Why? Because it seems hard to experience love when shame is present, so in these moments when you meet yourself with love through a self-soothing hug, through hugging another, it feels good to stop and honor that moment.

Please note that shame is an emotion that tells you that you are unworthy or worthless, and that creates isolation, and then we sit in shame. My call, my invitation is to self-soothe in a healthy way and to invite your community in for support.

Movement items: Place this work in your notebook (or the space provided on the next page if adequate for you), answer them aloud if you can, and bring this work to your community as well. There's a later chapter that will explain why we need to take this to our community in great detail.

Two Loving Yourself Properly Movement Items

Discover your most common shame-based phrases or thoughts. (What are they? Where did they come from? Write them down below or in your personal notebook for introspection and review.)

What are some ways of thinking or phrases that offer you more love, compassion, or understanding for your journey in life?

It's important that you recognize this by simply asking the question *how do I love myself better?* You are doing that just by asking the question. Self-awareness is the ability to observe yourself without judgment and without shame. As we travel down the rabbit hole of pondering what self-love is and isn't, let us do so without shaming our journey; and also, let's recognize that we already are doing enough.

I've found that one of the key practices for this to work is to find your breath. Finding your breath truly means focusing on your breathing, allowing your entire presence of mind to shift to your breathing, feeling the air go in and out of your lungs, listening to your body as you take in fresh air, and exhaling whatever energy needs to exit as you empty your lungs. Take a minute or so to breathe deeply and to acknowledge that you are asking the right questions, and that, for this moment, is more than enough. Here are two affirmations that you can repeat aloud after finding your breath.

At this moment, **I am enough**.

I am so happy and grateful for my body. I am so proud of who I am today. I am enough as I am; I've learned to accept myself, to love my life for what it is and this feeling has lifted my spirits. I'm grateful for this recognition.

— Sylvester McNutt III • I am enough

I affirm that I will not do any fake positivity under the muse of self-love. Yes, I do want to love myself and others, but I'll be honest and admit that, on some days, I don't have my best stuff. When this happens, I want to show up as my true and honest self. I deserve happiness that is genuine, and my sorrow deserves a sacred space to exist as well.

— Sylvester McNutt III • I am enough

Self-Love Season

I affirm that this season of
my life is about loving myself
properly, and I'll take my time as
I learn how to listen to my wants and
needs. I am learning how to honor what
I want and what I need, and this is a sacred space
that I will meet with compassion and patience, daily.

— Sylvester McNutt III • Self-Love

THE BEAUTY IN SUMMER'S STORY AFTER THE WINTER FAILURE

When I was studying for a Bachelors of Arts from Northern Illinois University, a professor told me that it's best to strictly define who you are as a human, especially as a writer. I said, "Why do we have to define who we are if who we are is constantly changing?" And her response was "Sylvester, we are not constantly changing. The only thing that changes is the feedback from the world." I cannot tell you if her response is genius, if it's manipulative wordplay, or if it's just a way to dismiss my line of questioning.

Either way, I've always thought about the *feedback from the world* response; it has always entangled my spirit into reflection and questioning. In fact, that specific phrase has stuck with me since my three-hundred-level poetry class at Northern Illinois University. I took that class in the first semester, which lasted from the last week of August to the first week of December.

My college was eighty miles west of Chicago, Illinois, in a small country town named DeKalb. Imagine a Walmart, a Dairy Queen, and a university smashed together in the middle of the cornfields—that was the college backdrop for my story. And of course, there were parties, lots of studying and plenty of those stories that make you realize that college is more than "just" an education. It's an initiation into adulthood, it's a field trip through emotions, and an adventure down socialization.

A Normal Winter Day in DeKalb

A normal winter day in Illinois attacked my fragile skin like it was irrelevant. The wind never made an apology for the way it would strike me as if I did something wrong to it. My relationship with Mother Earth went to a new level during those college days, and it was when I realized that she was one of the most powerful entities in our lives.

Walking to class always felt like a punishment. It would be ten degrees below zero, and the snow would be frozen into the cracks of the streets. I loved writing, and I loved this class as well. It was a three-hundred-level poetry course, and man, did it spark up things that were brewing in my soul. I always made it to this writing class; that was how much I loved it, so much so that I would deal with abuse from the elements every day to get there, ha!

I felt challenged but seen in this class, even though my professor didn't see me for how I saw myself; she saw me as something different, something more potent but wild. I felt like my work was never enough and was always criticized. I would even say I was treated unfairly among the other students, but I do not have concrete evidence for this claim, but I do have a hunch that she was being unfair to me, even until this day. My only evidence was the intuitive feeling I had for the heat she applied to me.

I ended up failing this class. I'll never forget seeing the *F* on my semester report card. I was shocked and devastated. I felt like less than nothing—I was pissed, and shameful, and confused. Shame came in and destroyed my creativity for a bit; it was a pure derailment of my identity. *My childhood dream of becoming a writer was never going to happen if I'm failing writing classes in college*, I thought.

THE TRANSITION

At that point, my entire sense of self was connected to my writing, to my private poetry books that I never showed anyone except for my girlfriend. I was on the college football team, living in an apartment for the first time, and dating one of the most popular and attractive girls on campus. But none of that defined me, if you will; they were how other people saw me. I saw myself as a writer, and that failing grade greatly disconnected me from the assumed identity that I had.

I was conditioned like most people are in this society. If I perform well, then I feel great about myself. And if I fail, falter, or stumble, then I will feel bad about myself *because I am the worst person of all time.* (This sentence was written with sarcasm; however, look at the structure.) This is exactly what I was teaching you earlier about recognizing shame-based sentence structure, and then you can see how you tell the story of your life. Remember, our journey here is to reimagine how we see our lives; our journey here is to examine how we are looking at the story of our life and how we are telling this to ourselves and others.

The recipe is ***I am + negative word or phrase*** that reflects actions, attitudes, standing in life, or behavior. Never forget this recipe. It's like a great taco recipe; once you learn it, you must remember how it's put together.

WHAT FAILURE FEELS LIKE

When your heart and soul is connected to something and then you fail, you lose, or you get feedback that tells you that you are unworthy of the connection, that moment can break you—if you believe it, of course. And when you're an amateur writer looking up to a writing professor who tells you that you aren't good enough, you allow your soul to die under her opinion. I'm sure you can change the characters around, and this story will fit you at one point or another.

It felt like half my skin melted off my skeleton, and my visual bones sat there singed from the heat. The pain of feeling my ego, my soul, and all my beliefs pass away can trigger the sharpest emotions. That failure, for me, was pain. Pain is so powerful that it can make you feel every emotion a human experiences, and at the same time, you feel numb and nothing at all. Damn.

The question becomes, then, as a writer, as a chef, as a manager, as a human resource person, as a mom, as a dad, as a son, as a daughter, as a human, how do we begin to love ourselves when we seek validation from others and when their validation acts as the permission slip for us to love ourselves? How do we begin to look at these common situations that occur in our lives, and what can we learn from them? Are we going to repeat and believe these shame-based phrases that keep us away from our highest self? Or, do we have the ability to grieve that moment and bounce back? You tell me.

REIMAGINE SUCCESS AND FAILURE

Reimagine how you view success and failure. It's crucial that we begin to examine what we individually view as success and failure, and we must begin to define what it means for our story, and also bringing our reactions into our waking consciousness. It's important to see that they are two sides of the same coin, too. Doing so will help us see that we must stop judging ourselves this way. Many of us worship the god of success, and my invitation here is to recognize how dangerous it is.

We are becoming aware of how we are choosing to see our life. We are looking at the question *how do I love myself?* The answer, no matter how deep or shallow, is nothing but an image. From the examples I have given about the young man who has failed college, if you peel each one back, you'll see that the young man who sat in those classes saw himself as nothing but a collection of images. We do this with our lives; that is why it is so essential that we use self-awareness techniques to observe what images we are choosing to see.

So my friend, who are you when you fail? Who are you when you succeed? Is it possible, that you are indeed the same person? Is that possible for you? If you are the same person then does that mean that in the near future you can practice a more mindful response to your failures and success. Need an example?

A writer puts out a book; it becomes a bestseller and impacts millions of readers worldwide. We would call that book a ***success***, which would bring emotions of happiness, bliss, and freedom. The writer does not need to feel like a failure or success but instead recognizes that this specific journey of his or her life is resulting in a ***successful project***.

Flip the story: the book bombs, the reviews are awful, and the book is a failure. Well, the human behind that project does not have to say self-defeating thoughts like, "I am a failure" because that's not true. The truth is that the ***project failed at this moment***, and that's all, and he or she is allowed to acknowledge that without shame.

We don't know about the past or the future for this person, and truthfully, neither matter. All we know is this moment is not a success because they experienced a failure, and it's okay to have that normal human experience. They're allowed to feel dejected, disappointed, and discouraged.

They're allowed to grieve, ask questions and reflect — but how long does one stay there?

Can we begin to reimagine ourselves as that young student. At the time, that boy failed his poetry class and he felt the pits of human emotion. He hated Professor Sommers for failing him that winter. He took his failure and the pain that came, and he internalized it alone. He chose to keep his community out. (Have you done this? Are you doing this? Is this self-love? Is this the best way to process shame and failure, or should we do it in community?)

We have to be careful with judgments and images of success and failure because they may be incomplete, and if we give either too much credit, it can lead to a critical inner voice, which is not what we want. We want to be encouraging, compassionate, and willing to experience all the shades of life.

That failed three-hundred-level poetry writer went on to become a self-published, best-selling author of multiple books. What if he stayed stuck on the image of what happened to him that winter? Loving yourself properly means that you'll allow yourself to see the full image, and if the whole picture is not there, you will give yourself compassion for what is present and you'll remain optimistic about what is possible. It means that you have to be patient and open to what may come. It's not about hoping for better, or praying that things will work out either. No, it's about being compassion about reality, about what is, about what is presently happening — that's where the healing is.

And then, when the time is right, it's about putting your armor on and going back to war and fighting for what's right, for your destiny, for your purpose.

Invitation to Movement

You have something inside you that has been muffled, and maybe it's because of a past failure, a past image—hell, even your success may be holding you back from what is calling you. If you are going to have an honest look at self-love, then you have to ask yourself to bring back those pieces of yourself that are calling you. Is it the piano that you used to play in junior high school or the dances you used to do with your sisters? Do you have a burning desire to do graphic design, but for some reason, you're not spending your time there? What about that part of you that wants to eat pizza from different countries until you find the best one?

I'm not saying it's going to be easy or hard — we don't know, and difficulty isn't our focus anymore. I am not saying you are going to make any money because you might not and hell, you might develop generational wealth from this thing, too — it's possible.

I am not saying that you will become a success or a failure — what if you become neither? I am saying that there are parts of you that you're hiding, that you aren't giving love to, that you are not allowing to love you; and if you want to love yourself wholeheartedly, that has to end today. I challenge you to get moving toward that thing that is calling you. Maybe it does mean switching jobs, leaving the country, or moving out of the house you've been in for twenty years. Maybe it means you need to get out a notebook, research and ask questions. Whatever that thing is that is calling you though, even if it's something like picking up your camera again you have to start today.

A calling is not something we can ignore. Maybe we weren't ready when we saw the call; maybe we became distracted and diluted. Well now the goal is to make ourselves potent adults, and we can only do that when we honor our callings.

In the image of the boy, however, he did something that we cannot do. He did it alone and in secret, and he kept everyone out. It caused him pain, the isolation hurt him, and the fact that he hid something he was passionate about caused him to feel like he was living a fake alternative life. He didn't allow himself to be seen, to be himself, until after a decade of being a full-time author; and if he could accelerate your journey faster than his, he would simply invite you to these words—do not do it alone.

Bring in your community on the new endeavor. They may not get it; they may not understand, especially if they never went for a calling, especially if they are ignoring that thing inside them that needs to be brought out. Tell your community about your calling, about your love, about your passion, about your images. Most people want something and someone to believe in, so why can't they believe in you?

And remember, this isn't about career, money, or validation from others. This challenge of movement is solely about allowing yourself to spend more time following a calling—the calling that you love—and if you do not know what that is, then it is time to explore. And as you explore, you collect images, ask questions, and listen to your body and mind. Listen to how you feel as you invest into what moves you, into what brings you love.

We are trained to look at success and outcomes as black and white. Today we must break up with that, and instead, we must look at the journey, the images, complete and incomplete; and most of the time, we must realize that we don't have enough images to see certain pictures clearly. Loving ourselves properly means allowing ourselves to go after the other images, to see life fully. This is why we should not jump to conclusions and write ourselves or anyone off just because of one image that is unclear.

Professor Sommers represents someone in your life who has created a shift in you. Maybe they don't believe or see your light, but you must use their energy as a motor. Sommers represents someone in your life who has inspired you to move into action. She is the people who need you to be potent so they can turn to you, so they can lean on you. The winter and summer teaches you every year that your environment changes, and so must you.

I do not believe that there is such a thing as failure; in fact, I've used the word twenty-eight times in this book to connect with common language, to penetrate your soul. However, we have to throw away the concept. It does not give us an accurate view of our life.

The entire concept of failure builds a limitation around who we can be, how we can tell our story, and the power that lives inside us. Do you want to limit yourself? Do you want to put a cap on who you can be? I don't believe you do; therefore you have to throw away this word and the concept of failure. From now on, let's speak on every event as an opportunity, as a lesson, as an action or inaction.

Throw away the idea that you are a failure, that you have failed, or that failure has any validity in your vocabulary or mindset. There is no such thing as failure. No matter what action you take, you will learn, there will be movement on something, and consequences will happen based on what you do and do not do.

Throw away the idea of failure and allow yourself to be human; allow yourself to live and learn. There is no such thing as failure—there is only what you learn or observe from a situation and what you do not.

Four Focuses to Recognize on Healing Shame

1. ***Recognize that you are not alone.*** Your shame wounds keep you from intimacy, from connection, from showing up fully in your community. Get more comfortable talking about your shame; others around you will notice your bravery, and they will follow suit. We all want to get rid of our shame, but we often don't until we feel safe. For us to feel safe, someone has to take the risk of being seen.

2. ***Recognize when you are isolating yourself.*** Shame wants you to sit in the dark basement alone; it chops off your nourishment, which is love, community, being witnessed, and the ability to live your life in full bloom.

3. ***Recognize when you are lying to yourself.*** You do this because you don't feel like you will be accepted (likely a result of previous pain or family structures that do not support full expression). As you attempt to heal shame, which is the first step to self-love, then you must recognize when you are lying to yourself.

4. ***Recognize when you use shame-based thoughts*** like *I am not good enough* and replace them with positive affirmations like "I am so grateful that I am in a position to learn more about this."

Recognize that you are not alone.
Recognize when you are lying to yourself.
Recognize when you are isolating yourself.
Recognize when you use shame-based thoughts
and replace them with words that heal you.

This is the perfect time for self-compassion,
to surround yourself around love and to challenge
yourself to treat yourself with as much love as possible.

Three Focuses to Recognize on "Failure"

1. ***Recognize that failure is needed.*** We live in a society that is obsessed with winning and losing, and we herald those who "win," and we shame those who "lose." We have to throw away that mindset and accept that failure is a part of the journey. How many times must we fall off the bike before we can finally ride it? We must begin to use the word *reps* more. *Reps* is short for "repetition." Life is a game of trial and error, and the more reps we have, the better.

2. ***You might not be good enough today, but that doesn't mean you should shame yourself.*** We become obsessed with the endpoint that we forget this is a journey. It's okay to not be ready, to not know enough, to not be good enough for something in this moment. Your script that was rejected may not be that good, this is true. It also may just need to be seen by five hundred more producers. Instead of staying down about failure, use it to fuel you—keep going.

3. ***Recognize when you hide your gifts because of fear.*** There are Grammy-level singers who only sing in the shower. There are best-selling authors who only write in their notes. There are gifts inside each one of us, and it is our duty to share, to be seen, to allow others to choose to participate in our gifts. You might be afraid and it's okay to have fear, and to still push through.

Recognize that failure is needed so give yourself a chance to fail, to learn from it and that is how you will succeed. You might not be good enough for the outcome you expect today, but that doesn't mean you should shame yourself or slow down your pursuit of what you crave. Instead, lean into learning, practice and asking questions. Recognize when you hide your gifts because of fear.

— Sylvester McNutt III • Failure Happens

Some people feel like they don't have purpose, and that tells me they still have not met their shame wound. Your shame is keeping you away from your purpose, and so it's time to move into it, to see it, to acknowledge it so the wound can heal.

Right now your purpose is deeply healing. Your purpose is to allow yourself to grieve, to be seen, to change the mindsets on who you are so you can be your true self. I acknowledge that this may be hard and takes time, but I hope you recognize that it's worth it.

— Sylvester McNutt III • Deep Healing

Shame wants you to hide who you are; it wants you to be invisible. But you matter, your smile matters, and you inspire people with your story. The world needs to hear from you, needs to see you, and needs to feel your energy.

Sylvester McNutt III • Let Us See You

There is nothing wrong with getting healthy solitude. Do that and heal. However, we are here to live in community, to be witnessed by others, to share sacred space with humans. Isolation is choosing to deal with pain, fear, and unruliness alone. Shame and pain love when you isolate because they grow there. Shame and pain cannot survive when you smother them with community and love and when you choose to be witnessed.

— Sylvester McNutt III • Deep Healing

We all have a calling, and you cannot ignore that calling any longer. Don't make this about money, fame, or validation. Your calling is something deep inside you that is saying "Cultivate me, practice me, allow me to unite with you."

Sylvester McNutt III • Embrace The Calling

I believe that every person has a gift that they need to offer the world. This gift serves two purposes: it gives the person purpose, and it gives value to the community. I believe we are meant to use our lives as practice to learn about the gift, to get better with it. And then we must present and offer our gift to others.

Sylvester McNutt III • You Have A Gift

When it comes to finding purpose, this focal point helps: **focus on health so we can live fully and feel the richness of life.** The jobs we take, the titles we have, and the people who know us will always be in motion. But health is something we need, and it's fragile if we neglect it. If you feel a lack of purpose, make your health a priority, and you'll feel new purpose flow through your life.

— Sylvester McNutt III • Healing Is Your Purpose

2

How to Destroy Limiting Beliefs

WHAT DO YOU WANT TO BE WHEN YOU GROW UP? I'm asking you. Say it aloud right now. What do you want to be when you grow up?

You might say, "But wait, I'm an adult already. I'm grown." Ha! No, you're not. As long as you have limiting beliefs, you are still a kid trapped in an adult's body. You are still the seven-year-old you who has some healing to do. You still have some mindset changes that need to happen before you grow up into your most favorite self. This was a freeing awakening that I had a few years ago, and my solution was to meet this recognition with kindness and compassion (offer yourself the same, friend).

We are not here to destroy our parents or our families because I'm confident that most of them are honestly doing the best they can with what they have, which is not the best use of our energy. Even if you are a parent now, I know that you are trying the best you can with what you have in the depths of my soul. I know I am as well, and honestly, being a parent can be challenging on some days. If you can find forgiveness in your heart for your parents, then you can free yourself from the limiting beliefs that they passed to you. If you choose to resent them, freeing yourself may be much more challenging.

I have so much respect for all our ancestors who tried to give us a better life. In some cases, our parents passed on to us limiting beliefs that usually live inside us forever. They hold us back from potential, from feeling the richness of life, from healing shame, from developing connections, from showing up in this world the way that we deserve, from having powerful sexual energy, from being confident when we talk. And the list goes on and on. My purpose is to disrupt the pattern—I'm here to help you throw away your limiting beliefs.

Let me share a story of how a limiting belief was created in me, and then I will tell you how to destroy them. First, take one minute to message me on Instagram directly, and tell me that you're on to chapter two. We live in one of the best generations, one where people can connect from all over the world, and I would love to hear from you!

PENNY AND KOBE

I grew up in Chicago in the 1990s, and my parents always watched the Chicago Bulls basketball games. Michael Jordan was king of the court, and the Bulls dominated sport and airwaves. Sports people love to argue who the best player of all time is, and I don't enter those conversations anymore. I find myself saying things like, "I am not about to sit here and argue with you about these multi-millionaires, ha." And that response usually shuts people up.

I had two favorite players growing up. First was Kobe Bryant, another author and Virgo. Kobe and I share the same birthday of August 23, and I felt a special connection to him and still do. The other player was named Anfernee Hardaway, but his nickname was Penny. Penny and Kobe were my favorite players because they both had a mindset that grabbed me as a young boy. That mindset was simple: *you can't guard me.*

Penny and Kobe were young players, so their teams were developing culture, but Jordan's teams had the championship culture already. They won six championships, and three of them were back to back to back. And at the time of this writing, that hasn't been done since.

When Michael Jordan was on the court, his mindset was to dominate you, to embarrass you, and to do whatever it takes to win. His belief system was that he was the better player and that his team was better than yours. Kobe Bryant, later in his career, developed the Mamba mentality, which had been labeled a killer instinct in the context of sports. Kobe was known for his work-ethic, his attention to detail on the court, and his tenacity. Again, I would call this his belief system. He believed that when he stepped on the court there wasn't a single person who could guard him, or beat his team. I would like to call it an unlimited belief system in self and in culture. Penny Hardaway was relentless; he was lean and mean. You could look in his eyes and see that he knew he was the best player in the universe.

These guys reached the level they did in their careers and postbasketball careers because of their mindset. Kobe went on to win an Emmy, become a published author, and be a compassionate father and husband. Michael Jordan went on to change the world as far as sneakers, culture, and business were concerned and even from a philanthropist standpoint by building hospitals and centers to help the community in North Carolina. Penny had a great career, and he returned home to Memphis to coach and instill that mindset in young men, and to be a mentor and elder to them. Penny went on to coach a bunch of success teams in at University ofMemphis. I don't know these guys personally, and I'm not saying any one of these men are perfect; however, I am saying that they do not have limiting beliefs — at least, not in the realm of basketball.

Can You Buy Me the Shoes?

As basketball culture exploded in the 1990s by the likes of Jordan, Kobe, Penny, and others, I found myself craving some attire just like all the other kids. I wanted the Kobe Bryant Crazy 8s that came out in 1998 and the Penny Hardaway series shoe that came out in 1995, and there was the Jordan 12s, which are infamous because that's when he dominated Utah in what has been called the "flu game."

For a kid, grabbing a pair of these shoes meant something, especially as a basketball fan. It meant that you were connected to your favorite player. It meant that you would play like your favorite player as well. I played basketball at the park every single day with my friends int he spring, fall and summer. I wanted to embody the energy of my favorite players before I consciously understood why.

When I brought the idea to my parents about getting these expensive shoes, the response was "No, you have gym shoes already. You don't know the value of money." And honestly there is nothing wrong with that answer. I'm grateful for all the hard work and sacrifices that my parents put forth to put me and my siblings in a position where we didn't have to worry if we were going to eat. We were not poor, and we were not rich. I wore my cousin's hand-me-down clothes since he was taller than me, and every now and then, my parents would go to a bargain shop for things like shoes, clothing, and bags. I can respect any parent who says no given that kids typically do not have an understanding of what it takes to buy a $200 pair of shoes; however, this moment created a self-defeating thought in me that stayed in me until I chose to examine my subconscious.

"You Don't Know the Value of Money"

Although it was an accurate statement for the person who said it to me, still, it's a self-defeating thought that ran rampant through my identity until I went to war with that mindset in adulthood. And had I been taught the value of money, then I would have known *how* to get what I wanted. Many of us were told no, and we weren't given the framework, energy, or encouragement to go for what we wanted, and as a consequence, we have developed a life of not pushing for what we want. Question: is that showing up fully to this life? Is that self-love? Is choosing a lesser version of yourself love? I can't answer this — I am just here to ask.

Your homework right now is to examine what self-defeating thoughts you have been given around money, your body, your intelligence, or any other pillar that we could insert here. And if they haven't been given to you, it's your job to simply ask, *What self-defeating and limiting beliefs do I repeat over and over that I should choose to let go of?*

I'm not a sneakerhead by any means, but I love training and having high-quality gear that only enhances the experience of training. Present day, I was in Scottsdale Fashion Square Mall, and I saw the exact same shoes that I wanted as a kid for the small price of $200. Yikes! The interesting thing is I didn't actually need the shoes because I already had a great pair of Adidas Ultraboost to work out in. The nice lady at Champs Sports said, "Sir, what can I help you with today?" I told her that I was just browsing, my automatic response so I could avoid yet another conversation about money.

I instantly walked away because I knew that I didn't need those shoes, and as I was walking away, I could hear the voice in my head say, 'You don't know the value of money." That little self-defeating thought just kept replaying over and over in my head. I begin to think to myself: how many times have I thrown away an opportunity or kept myself living small because I choose to repeat the limiting belief system that my parents unknowingly gave me? As soon as I recognized the thought and became aware of the consequence of the thought pattern, I shifted into a new opportunity. I choose to let go of the old thought so a new opportunity and emotion could unfold right in front of me. I turned back around and went to the lady who was helping me.

I looked at those all-white Penny Hardaway shoes with blue trim and the deep blue sole, and I instantly thought about the child version of me. I thought about that little boy who naively asked for an experience, and energy exchange and I knew that it was time for me to serve him. I said, "I want to get these; size 11. Can you bring them to the register, please?"

"Let me go to the back and make sure we have them. I'll be right back."

They had the shoes; I paid for them without trying them on, and went home. I bought those shoes as a gift to the child in me, solely with the intention of letting him know that he does know the value of money. Solely with the intention of breaking up with that old mindset that no longer guided me towards me detest love, and that energy exchange in the store represented that.

Question: what self-defeating thoughts are you holding on to? Think on this and journal on it before you continue.

Reroute—Healing Ritual

When I got home, I went into my closet and tried the shoes on—they were a perfect fit. I had a small but powerful conversation with my child self, and I said, "I honor you, I see you, and I want you to know that you will learn the value of money, and you will have more than enough to do anything you want in life. Money will flow through you. You will be wealthy, and you will change your family tree. Don't feel guilty when you do something for yourself. You have enough to take care of everything that's important, and you have enough to have fun and enjoy your money. Money is a tool and you will develop a healthy relationship with this tool." And then all the shame that I had around money began to vanish. That moment, and following conversation was an initiation into new possibilities and new energy.

This process is what I like to call a reroute. A route is what? It's a destination or path that takes a person from point A to point B; the word alludes to something traveling over a distance. What if we are trying to move on from low self-worth to high self-worth? How do we do it? What if we want to move on from little confidence to an abundance of confidence?

NO SELF-HATRED

No matter what you are looking to change, you cannot do it with self-hatred; you have to honor the past and present versions of yourself. Don't look at that seven-year-old you who lives inside you with contempt because, then, there will not be a safe container for love, for growth, for getting a new image for what's possible. Make sure you look at your past and present selves with compassion; that is your number one tool on this journey of giving and honoring your old self so those old, unhelpful mindsets can die—and this takes time.

Our work here—and this is hard but necessary—is to listen deeply to our voices and thoughts and to attack and truly investigate them so we can be fully aware of what subconscious thoughts may be limiting us from the life we deserve. Those thoughts given to us that do not push us to where we need to go must be given the space to die. We have to grieve those thoughts and honor that they have been helpful because they probably have helped us survive, and then we have to bury them. I suggest saying them aloud and then stating over and over, "These thoughts no longer align with me." Words are power, and that is how we abolish thoughts that no longer serve us.

"These thoughts no longer align with me." I say that over and over any time I feel a voice creeping in that no longer serves my mission. This is about changing our language, and once we do, then we switch our capacity. We change the space that is available to our journey. This small and simple practice is also a grief ritual as it creates space to honor and accept change.

If you are on a healing journey and you want to do 'more', then by all means, do more; but before you do, all I ask is that you sit down and allow yourself to become fully aware of your limiting beliefs. If you have been told that you're not worthy of buying, seeing, or feeling a particular experience, I want you to challenge that. Maybe you didn't perform well sexually one time for an ex, and now you refuse to have sex because you don't want to deal with the shame and potential embarrassment. I'm here to let you know that you can safely experience that exchange; it's possible.

Maybe you got cut from an athletic team in high school, and now you don't work out, even though you know you should because you don't feel strong enough. I want you to know that there's a trainer or coach, and a potent community of people who are not judgmental, and all they want to do is welcome you into the world of finding what training style works for you.

Maybe you came from a home where there was abuse, neglect, and constant disconnection, and now you don't trust anyone. I see you, I hear you, and I want you to know that there are people who want to love you, who would love to know you, and don't intend to hurt you at all. We are worthy of entering and working on healthy relationships, but we have to believe this, and we have to trust that this is available to us—because it is.

The game we are playing is about investigating our thoughts and then detaching ourselves from them, especially the ones that bring us into a lower vibration and a poorer quality of life. This practice brings us fully into the present, into a place where we are not judging and critiquing ourselves; this practice brings us into a silence—a silence that we've needed for so long. The majority of the noise that we hear is not our voice, and our practice here is carving the space so we can finally here our own loving, beautiful, and majestic voice. When you talk about yourself always use love and compassion with every breath.

— Sylvester McNutt III • Loving Voice

WHY YOU NEED TO REROUTE YOUR THOUGHTS

- If 90 to 95 percent of our thoughts are happening at the subconscious level, then that means that, at some point, we have to investigate them. Otherwise, they will flow without restriction, and that causes us to live life on autopilot. If our life is not exactly what we want, that means there are thoughts we've allowed to pass without restriction.

- Self-defeating thoughts and limiting beliefs are always allowed to live inside your framework and your value system until you decide to honestly investigate those subconscious thoughts. Yes, this is hard, but we do not focus on what is hard; we must focus on what is necessary.

- Most people want to do more to get the results they want. The truth is 'more' is not going to get us in the direction we need to go if our belief system is holding us back. More doesn't have a purpose if our inner thoughts are that *we are not good enough*, *we are unworthy*, and *no matter how we show up, it's just not enough*. Instead of focusing on doing more, ask yourself if you can separate from your self-defeating thoughts.

- You cannot control every aspect of life; however, you can greatly influence which thoughts you choose to keep. Those make up your framework for how you behave, and your behavior creates your lifestyle.

- You can manifest your future through your present thoughts. Your thoughts become your actions, and your actions are the only thing you can control in life. Never complain about your life because that negative energy will bring you into a lower vibration. Instead, adjust your thoughts to align with the actions needed to create your desired outcomes.

I'm Afraid of Getting Rid of My Limiting Beliefs; What Should I Do?

- If you know that you have self-defeating thoughts and you choose to empower them, then you are choosing to do life small and hidden, and your soul will burn you up until you are engulfed. Your soul came to this life for full participation, and it is going to fight so that can happen.

- If your fear is that you will lose connection with friends, family, and people you've known, you're right, that's possible. It's also possible that they need an example of what it looks like when someone says, "Enough. I came here to live my life fully." Maybe your job is to show them and yourself what's possible.

- Throwing away self-defeating thoughts on your own may be hard and, for some, impossible, but you know that you have to break up with them. Use this as an invitation to do the journey with a therapist. Let your therapist know that you want to participate fully in your life and that your self-defeating thoughts are holding you. They will work with you, and they'll hold a space for you.

- Think about all the hardships and struggles that your

ancestors went through. Do you think they would want you to keep yourself small, to believe in limiting and self-defeating thoughts? Or do you think they would want you to move deep into your happiness, your purpose, your worthiness?

Allow Yourself to Feel Worthy of Abundance

Every single person reading this book has a current limiting belief that holds him-or herself back from the desired life they seek. Our work here is to bring that limiting belief directly into our consciousness and to hold it, to see it —is that limiting belief also rooted in some deep shame wound? If so, I see you, I hear you, and I understand how hard it can be due to the entanglement of shame and the limiting belief. Our work is to abolish all limiting beliefs. We do not allow love to come in fully, we block ourselves from deep connection, from laughter, from joy, from presence, and we play small if we allow limiting beliefs to circle around our frameworks.

How To untangle shame & limiting beliefs?

The great thing about this paradigm is that choosing to focus on making peace with one or the other helps get rid of both. This is one of the rare occasions where you can get a "buy one get one free." I'll use italics to help illustrate for you how this works. Take a look at this sentence structure below:

"*I probably won't be a best-selling author* because my *work isn't as good* as Mr. X."

That sentence is not helpful to us. The phrase *I probably won't be a best-selling author* is a limiting belief, and the words *because I am not as good as Mr. X* are where shame is inserted. The truth is, to have the life we want, to have self-love, we have to get out of the comparison game. Mr. X can no longer be our ceiling or our floor; comparing ourselves with his journey will not help us at all. Our work here is to ignite our soul, to lock ourselves into a life of passion, to see the beauty in living. How can we ever achieve that if we are allowing other people to be our benchmark for judging what our soul needs us to do in this life?

When you sit on the porch in a thunderstorm, what do you see? You see a chorus of beautiful lightning bolts dancing across the sky; you hear the echo of thunder as it reverberates across the soil. The lightning bolts just move and meander based on the energy of the moment. And you sit there and watch the show, fully engaged and aware. That is what we have come here to do. We are the lighting; we are the sky, the soil. We, if we choose to be are highly abundant and potent people—but we have to choose this.

So how is that sentence supposed to go? It should sound like this: "I am a best-selling author, and my work has influenced millions of people. I write books that change people's lives, that help them see their potential, and that challenge people to stride in their deepest authenticity. My authorship inspires other writers to respect the words, to respect the readers, and to give his or her dedication to the project. My work holds value in the real world and leaves people feeling seen, loved, and held properly. My work comes from a genuine place and I am grateful for the opportunity to share."

So, my friend, which of those statements sounds better? Which one ignites you? Which statement gives you purpose and clarity? Which statement begs you to engage? Which statement will you use for your life, with your story moving forward? You must choose.

Of course, the latter one, and that is how we must talk about our journeys. We must begin to see the abundant nature in which the world exists. The world has always had abundance, and even with man taking and taking, there's still plenty for us.

Use Positive Affirmations To Support And Encourage Your Day-To-Day Energy

Saying positive affirmations can feel *wrong* if you are used to saying affirmations that destroy your energy. You can feel like an impostor if the words do not currently align with how you actually feel. In the *Loving Yourself Properly* framework, one thing I need you to accept is that two things can be true at the same time.

Often we are taught to think in a limiting way that there's

one view, one choice, or one thing on and one thing off. You can be working on yourself, and you can already be exactly where you are supposed to be; those can both be true. You can be worthy of success even if you are still learning, growing, and building your business or self. You can be worthy of entering and maintaining fruitful relationships even if you are intensely focused on discovering yourself; there is a powerful unexplainable duality that is always present.

You can be worthy of earning an athletic scholarship even though you're not playing your best, even though your grades may be down this semester — you can still do it. You can be a future parent who is present, loving, and inspiring even though you are deep into your studies and focusing on yourself. Two things can be true at the same time, and what makes them true is our thought process and belief system.

I will argue greatly that we have to be aware of our thoughts, especially limiting ones because those love to connect with shame; and once that happens, it turns into Gorilla Glue on our self-image. We get locked into the wrong things, images, and behaviors that take us away from our desired goals and the energy needed to actualize the life we deserve.

Your homework today is to get a journal and write down all your limiting beliefs. Dump them all out of you and place them directly onto that paper. I want you to feel them leaving your body as you write them down. What you're going to do is a small but powerful ritual. Whatever you write down, go ahead and read it aloud and become aware of the words. If you are this intentional, you'll see that you don't energetically like how those words feel. If the words you're looking at are not going to help you get toward self-love, healing, abundance, or living the beautiful life you deserve, then you have to throw those words away right now.

Speak aloud exactly what you want. Even if you don't 100 percent align with it, you have to still speak it because words have a vibration and an energy that your mind and body will recognize. This is why you must specifically say what you want, and you must say it over and over. Using words this way is actually you calling yourself into your highest power.

The 2.0 gpa student who wants to get a 3.5 gpa this semester can do it if he or she changes his or her belief system. Why? Because, new beliefs will create new energy and new possibility, which will then create new outcomes.

"I am worthy of a 4.5, and I will do the work." That type of declaration and energy is what moves you. This is the genesis of self-love: it's seeing that how you talk to yourself is the main power, and the first sign of resistance is often shame and limiting beliefs. And once those are unlocked, it becomes one hundred times easier to move into purpose, healing, passion, and seeing the aesthetics of life.

I will argue that if we want to bring the deepest form of self-love into our life, then at the same time we must become fully aware of what we think and what shames us. And then we can begin to cook that material. We have all the material we need, but we haven't found the right container until now. You, right now, are the perfect container; otherwise, you would not see these words, and you would not be asked to be this intentional.

You are the power, and the energy that you need is flowing through you.

Do that ritual today; do not skip it. Hold yourself accountable and get those words out of your body. To complete the ritual, write yourself a new list of words that describe who you are and what you want out of life. This list can always be changed and can be adjusted as you see fit; you are not limited here. We can do this practice every single day until we create the genuine energy we need to propel us in to our favorite self.

Energy is everything — get in the habit of speaking on precisely what you want out of life. And then, take massive action towards what you want, and repeat the cycle.

Talk about it and then act on it. Get in the practice of being in one hundred percent alignment with precisely what you do desire. This practice creates more intentional energy for the path that you desire most.

— Sylvester McNutt III

3

Moving Into Shame Wounds

AS WE BEGIN TO LEAN INTO MORE powerful imagery, thoughts, and ideas about our lives, we can find different points of resistance.

For some, we are only going to love ourselves properly once we learn to live with or get rid of our shame. We need the right container and the right focus to do it, but we must move into our shame wounds so we can unlock the love that is awaiting us during the process.

Oftentimes you only get something once you come out on the other end. When it comes to shame, that's not true; you begin to get more love the second you lean into shame, the second you acknowledge it, the moment you begin to see yourself as a human who is allowed to simply be that. Once you admit and simply become aware of your shame, you gain love instantly because you are not self-sabotaging, self-ignoring, or bypassing anymore. That taste in the air is freedom — freedom via the choice of objective observation and genuine acceptance.

I want you to finish this sentence: when I think about ___________ , I recognize that is my shame. I'm so pumped up about this line—this line is the path to freedom. I had to do this several times while writing this book. I wanted to investigate and discover my shame. I ended up losing twenty pounds while writing this book. Why? Because I let go of shame and I let it go by facing it. My consequence is that my lifestyle changed and aligned seamlessly, that is why the twenty pounds left my body (not to say that one must lose weight). Once I faced it, then I was able to examine how I was living. I brought in more love with better habits, boundaries, and less stress and made my life easier. One of my many sentences was "When I think about my relationship to food and, in particular, snacking, I recognize that is my shame."

On the day that I said this out loud, I was finally able to feel lighter emotionally, which helped me become lighter physically. I said it to my network, and then my life started forming around metabolizing and cooking my shame. I stopped using phrases like "cheat meal" because they create shame, keeping me stuck in a cycle. Cheating has a negative connotation, and every time I would "cheat," I would feel the consequence of that belief system.

I began to recognize that food is fuel, and hell, it's even fun at times. Instead of "cheating," I accepted that I could enjoy all aspects of life as long as I use my boundaries. In my situation, my boundaries meant portion control, having whole foods, fiber, protein, carbs, healthy fats, and allowing myself never to feel bad for enjoying the snacks that I do. Instead of getting the unhealthy snacks from the gas stations, I started getting them from the local organic grocery store, and then, after practice, I started making them at home. This lifestyle change changed everything energetically, but I recognized my shame and disrupted the mental patterns. I was able to get rid of unnecessary body fat, put on muscle, and still eat snacks. Why? The energetic story changed. I defined what my boundaries had to be moving forward and became aware of shameful language and patterns. Look into your life now, and recognize where shame may be keeping you in a pattern.

Today is the day that we begin to wiggle free. It takes time because we are practicing the art of disruption here. We are trying to disrupt a pattern that may be interlaced with shame, which takes time but is worth it.

Always Remember, a Wound Heals

I see a shame wound as beautiful thing — it means we are alive, we are human. Once we can identify it, we can create the safe container for it to be healed, and that to me is beautiful. Some of us have not brought any attention to our shame, and that is why it has never healed.

Imagine playing baseball, getting a cut on your forearm, and never paying attention to the cut just to continue to play the game. No, we won't do that. We have to stop and acknowledge the wound. With a physical wound, we typically place some healing ointment on it and bandage it up to protect it, and then we wrap it so no other debris or dirt can get in there to make it worse. With our shame, we haven't done that. That changes today; it's time to pause and put a bandage on our shame wound. It's time to acknowledge it so we can heal, so we can begin to feel full again.

The right target here is to slowly choose to move step by step into the wounds, to create the container for healing.

As you start to get closer and closer to facing and healing shame, you'll notice confidence that you didn't have before. You'll see friends and family in a different light because you'll see shame laced in their behaviors and phrases. You'll see people you know holding themselves back simply because of shame. And as you stay committed to doing this work, what happens is you become the beacon for others to lean on—simply because you choose to share your shame to make a container for it to live in.

And last, you might never get rid of your shame, and that's just being a realist. But if you take the time genuinely and care to make a container for it, it may not have the power it once did. And that feels like the right target—to safely minimize it and then, when ready, to destroy the shame.

Stand Tall and Face the Shame

Challenge: Tell someone close to you about your shame wound today. What is your shame? I suggest you write it down in a journal and be honest. And then also talk to someone about it. Every single person may not need to know, but some do; you know who you can trust (more people than you even realize when it comes to the conversation). Use your most genuine discernment for who you create this space with.

Why take this challenge and tell someone else about your shame? Why write about it in a notebook?

Because it needs to cook; it needs to be metabolized, and you cannot do all this in your head, in your body, alone—you cannot continue to seek healing only through yourself. The shame needs to cook, and the only way it will is if you get it off your body and into the universe. If you are not ready to speak face-to-face with a friend or partner, then hire a professional. If you have to wait to get in his or her appointment books, just know that the ocean is always available, jungles are waiting to hear the echoes of your voice, the night sky that is far away from the city is craving your heat. We have forgotten that we have nature and the cosmos to heal, to connect with as well. Sitting next to the ocean, alone, can bring you a great deal of clarity if you choose. We are nature and nature is us; use nature, too.

I define *shame* as a daunting feeling that is overwhelming and sometimes emotionally paralyzing laced with "I am not worthy and not good enough" energy; it's a feeling that makes us feel we are abnormal or that parts of us are strange or defective, and that make us unlovable or unacceptable. Shame is the minimization of our soul, the dulling of our passions; it is the catalyst that blocks us from showing up fully in our life. Our work here has to be about making space for shame, welcoming it, asking questions around it, talking with our friends and family about it, and recognizing that this society will not do this for us. However, we are a "society," so we have to do it for ourselves.

This journey may be messy, triggers may come up, and it may ignite many big emotions. I will argue that ignition is progress and is necessary, especially in places where there is dullness. The ignition is a signal that we are looking in the right direction, and as the Buddhists say, it shows us that we have the right view.

We need heat. We need to cook these ideas. When we choose to bring our shame to this cooking process, we allow it to enter the *nigredo*, a term first created by the alchemists that means "a blackening" or "to be cooked."

When it comes to shame and other unruly emotions, you begin to think that only you have this experience, which is not accurate (this is a symptom of shame). You think you are the only person dealing with it, but you're not. Shame has this isolating power, and it blocks you from conversation, intimacy, and openness—all things we need to experience the richness of human life.

That is why the *Loving Yourself Properly* framework is asking you to bring yourself out of isolation—to create a safe vessel for the shame wound. Shame needs to be a community conversation, and to me, that is the only way you can be fully seen—this is why your challenge for today is to have a shame conversation with someone in your community. And please note, it does not have to be dark and scary, look at the conversation as a simple safe release of energy for both people. Allow people in on the process. This helps you and them; it helps the community's entire potency. One of my favorite teachers has a quote that I'll never forget, here it is: "Where shame is present excitement is not."

—Francis Weller

It's essential that you face your shame wounds. Odds are shame is the most significant barrier to feeling the self-love you desire. And once you meet that shame wound with compassion and light, an energetic shift will occur in you. Meeting your shame wounds with compassion will introduce more love and self-compassion into your life. Your life will be a perpetual cycle of feeling like you are living your most authentic life. The relationships you have will deepen their capacity — all as a consequence of creating a safe vessel to process shame. **The people who love you now and in the future will always want you to be yourself.** Today, your work is to practice being your most authentic self, so that version of you shows up repeatedly. People want to see you in all your faces, even the ones that you practice hiding. Today is the day to embrace yourself fully — your dark and your light, create a safe acknowledgement for your shame wound and you will feel freedom ring.

—Sylvester McNutt III • Full Embrace

Fall in love with being your most genuine self. Shame may ask you to hide who you are, but that is not what love wants. Love wants you to be full, to be you, to be real so that love can bring in everything that you deserve. Love is the engine that drives you towards the most aligned life. Use love, examine shame so it doesn't use you.

—Sylvester McNutt III • Use Love

One of the best feelings ever is bringing your pain to a community of people who care about you. One of the worst feelings is keeping your pain on you and expecting your body to metabolize it on its own. I want to invite you to a space where you allow others to help you, to hold you, to guide you. You do not have to process pain alone, and the beautiful thing about it is once you choose to let others help you, you'll see all the love in your life.

—Sylvester McNutt III • Use Love

The love that is inside you is bigger than any pain or shame. Your work is to not only honor your shame and to thank it for keeping you safe but to also unlock all the love that you're allowed to feel, to see, to experience. Allow yourself to fully acknowledge and make a safe space to process the shame so you can hold on to more love. Use your imagination to wonder what life would be like if you fully embraced, without judgment, all of you.

Sylvester McNutt III • More Love

How to Have a Shame Conversation

1. ***Be direct and ask for participation; be gentle.***

Be honest and state your objective. "I want to have a conversation about my _________ (name the shame), o you have the capacity for that?" They may have the energetic capacity; they may not. Your focus here is on asking for participation. If you get a no back, that is okay. Keep trying until you find the right container for this conversation. You are not asking for permission to share because you already have that. You are seeking participation from someone who has the space for you — there's a big difference there.

2. ***Give permission.***

Tell the other person that they, too, can share their shame with you and that you are here to listen to them as well. This creates safety. And, note, they may need to have a different conversation and if you have the energy for that then let them know. Knowing that two or more people have agreed to enter this space, to co-create a safe vessel should ease tensions and fear around the conversation as a consequence it makes the conversation *easier.*

3. ***Build your boundaries for the conversation.***

Listen to your wants and needs. You may need to get it all out of your chest before the other speaks, or maybe you want them to ask questions and pick your brain. When it comes to your shame, you have to speak up on your wants and needs. I find it most helpful to share and then remain open for follow-up questions but you may want to bounce ideas off of each other as you share. Self-awareness is key here. Do you need to vent, get it off your chest and just be heard? Do you need a conversation where a person is asking questions? Do you need someone who shares their story too? If possible, communicate what you need.

4. ***State honestly and directly, "This is my shame wound that I am healing."***

The power of being direct feels so good, and in a way, it frees you. When you look for the right or the politically correct way to say things and you stumble over words and thoughts, honestly that sounds like a product of shame. It seems like you are afraid to say what is genuine to you at the moment. Maybe for you, the feeling is "I am tired of self-sabotaging my own success. It pisses me off and makes me feel like a fuckup." If that's how you feel, for once in your life (especially if you have a safe container), say how you feel.

5. ***End with touch.***

Touch is love, especially if touch is safe and wanted. If possible, end the conversation with a hug, handshake, or kiss (whatever is appropriate based on the context of the relationship).

And if you are doing a long-distance conversation, then self-soothe, hug yourself, rub your temples, or pat yourself on the chest. Please note that having this conversation may not be possible with certain people, and that is okay. A psychotherapist should have the framework, empathy, and capacity to create a container for you if you do not have that in friends or family.

And, touch may not be a reasonable outcome, and we can't expect others to hold that space for us. However, if it is, please use it and honor the sacred gift of touching, leaning on someone, and sharing safe conversational spaces. It's a gift to enter a conversation that feels good even if the topics are not our favorite at the moment.

How to Face Your Shame

- Don't allow it to be private.
- Don't act like it's not there.
- Don't pretend to be strong enough.
- Do attack the nemesis.
- Do pull others up with you.
- Do choose loving language.

Don't allow it to be private

Shame is an attack against the self in which the person believes they will be unaccepted by others. It feeds on others' opinions, so it makes sense that a person who feels shame will want to hide from everyone.

A person who feels shame expects condemnation from everyone. So it's important to note that shame is fed in isolation, but being in connection with others and receiving empathy and understanding are what begins to heal our shame. If our instinct is to hide and do our best to be invisible, then to heal is to practice being seen, heard, felt and recognized.

Don't act like it's not there

If you practice ignoring parts of yourself, you will not feel authentic. You'll always feel the fear of being "found out" by someone, and it could lead you to force out a pseudopersonality that's not *you* (the performer). Putting up any performance is exhausting and is draining, so what happens if you began to accept yourself fully? What happens if you began to breakup with the performer in you so you can be your most authentic self?

Don't pretend to be strong enough

Strength is a hard thing to measure but it's a word that is easy to use. Sometimes a person has the confidence to conquer their fears; at other times, they're barely holding on.

To pretend to be strong stems from wanting to stop being (or feeling like) a target. If we believe that we are a target, then we often put up a cloak of strength — for many different reasons. If there is a genuine threat, then yes, this strategy makes sense.

But if the person or situation is not a threat, then there's no justification for faking strength when what we genuinely need is support and guidance, and to be witnessed. We must realize that by not faking strength, someone can help us, hold us, teach us, guide us. Throw away the idea that you need to always be 'strong', especially if it is blocking you from learning, growing or evolving.

Do attack the nemesis

Myths, religions, rituals, and fairy tales tend to have personified energy forces to defeat, avoid, or get past, and the predatory supernatural being is almost never human. I call it a nemesis not as a judgmental description but to describe how it acts—predatory. Everyone will encounter this nemesis energy to some capacity. The confrontation is mandatory.

Trust that your nemesis is the agent challenging you to do what scares you the most. Walk toward the place you least want to go—into authenticity, into being seen again. We cannot be passive with the nemesis, why? Because there's not enough energy in being passive — so we must create the vessel of safety for this journey and attack it.

Do pull others up with you

You will make it to the other side of shame, and I consider that to be a privilege. You must use the privileges you have to bring up your community. Why not help people who struggle with shame understand the connection between their thoughts, emotions, and behaviors since you have experience and perspective? With your walk through shame, you could pull someone else along with you and help them focus on thoughts that typically go unnoticed, such as "I don't deserve happiness."

Do choose loving language

Through compassionate thought training, you can shift what the inner voice sounds like. If you are highly self-critical person, then practice loving language to become more accepting of yourself.

If you're dealing with shame, it means you need to have your story heard—the full and truthful story. It means you need to be witnessed, seen, and held properly.

And the actual story of your life is not all darkness; there are some chapters of light as well. Shame tells you that revealing your secret will only lead to more significant pain and darkness and that's not true.

The people who love you will be honored that you have chosen to trust them enough to confide in them. Lovingly tell your story and honor it. Always tells your story with love and compassion, even if you are telling a piece that you're not proud of — always tell your story with a loving tone. As you practice this you'll notice that shame won't be able to build up on new stories. Why? Because you're using empathy and compassion at the core of your stories.

Phrases to Say to Help Another Person Face Their Shame

"Thank you for your strength in what you shared with me."
"Thank you for sharing something so vulnerable with me."
"I am not here to judge you. I am here to witness you."
"You faced your shame earlier, and I want you to know that I see your effort, and I am deeply proud of you."
"I am here to support you in however you need it."
"I am proud of you."

The phrase "I am proud of you" matters. Use it with people you love often. Use it with yourself. Use it and mean it. "I am proud of you." Start telling yourself and others around you about why you are proud. It feels so good to hear someone say that they are proud of you. For some people, these words can be more powerful than an "I love you," especially if it's genuine.

—Sylvester McNutt III • I Am Proud Of You

Isolation Is Not the Same as Solitude

I don't know about you but I love alone time. I find it to be such a healing, restorative and necessary time to recharge my energy and to not have to absorb or manage any other human's energy. But it must be purposeful because I also love my community and creating beautiful experiences with others.

Isolation is not the same as solitude; isolation occurs because of pain, because you want to hide, because you want to withdraw. Isolation is ignoring or bypassing the conflict that is present in your life because it feels too hard or too painful to deal with. Solitude is healing and warm; it is done to charge or recharge. Solitude is choosing to be alone, safely knowing you have others to talk to and to spend time with. One of the overarching themes and principles in *Loving Yourself Properly* is that we are meant to be witnessed in a community, and we may have multiple communities that are containers for different experiences.

Isolation does not help you heal—in fact, it becomes a breeding ground for contempt, envy, jealousy, and unruly emotions. Isolation is where shame grows. It's where thoughts of unworthiness run rampant. And to be clear, solitude 100% can help you heal. Well, Sylvester, if I'm alone in both situations what is the major difference in once word? Great question, and the best answer I could give is here: intention.

Why Do We Isolate

The reason we isolate is that we feel defective or unworthy because of what we are going through or went through. We feel like what we are going through is a burden, and what's the point of sharing a burden with people? Or on the deeper level, we feel like the people in our lives now are the reason for our pain, so we grow more distant or choose isolation to get away from them. So we hide from others, and years of hiding under the muse of safety also create years of suppressing our art, our touch, our singing, our play, our fun —all the things that add to vitality and meaning.

We also isolate to get away from unsafe environments, unsafe people and to escape certain patterns and behaviors. Let me be clear, I am not saying that isolation is bad or wrong, I am just asking you to be very aware of what you are choosing.

How to Stop Isolating

First, I want you to know that I see you, I'm holding you, and I'm honoring that this can be tough. I was a person who chose to withdraw and to isolate because that felt safer, that felt easier. In the long run, you end up hiding and never nurturing the richness of life. When you hide and isolate, you keep all your gifts away from the world. Honestly we don't know you, the most genuine you—and we need to. To stop isolating, you have to choose to be seen, you have to choose to live in a community, and you have to stop keeping your problems to the walls of your apartment or house. Yes, you will have to integrate this part of you that wants to be hidden into the full image of you. Yes, one of the consequences of accepting this challenge means that you will have some tough conversations that will be uncomfortable. Objectively, observe this mood board I came up with, and feel free to add more language to it.

Mood Board for the Person Who Isolates (Shame Does This)

"I can't trust anyone."

"Me against the world."

"I can do this on my own."

"I can't do that, so I won't go."

"I'm always messing things up."

"My family does not accept me."

"No matter what I do, it's not enough.

"I'm not good at this, so I won't try it."

"I am not good enough, so I won't try."

"I don't need a man. They're all the same."

"I don't need a woman. They're all the same."

"I don't connect with my family. I'm not like them."

"My family thinks I'm crazy because I'm not like them."

What is the consequence of treating yourself with loving kindness and offering yourself compassion for any *mistakes* that you may have made? Imagine if you did this daily. How would you feel? Would this practice add value to your life in a positive manner?

—Sylvester McNutt III • Self-Love

Dear Self,

I will not allow myself to play small anymore. I am free from the stories of yesterday that trapped me, slowed me, or keep me in a story that no longer aligns with me. I am stepping into my most authentic power, my most loving voice, and into who I am. I embrace and love myself fully now — I am free and I am allowing myself to embrace the richness of life.

—Sylvester McNutt III

HOW TO ACCEPT THE RICHNESS OF LIFE

Because you have shame, which is a reflection of the thought *I am defective*, it becomes tough to accept the richness of life. Our work here is about untangling those words because they are lies, and our work is about allowing those phrases and thoughts to fade. The catch-22 here is that a person with shame does not want to be seen, but the solution is that they have to allow themselves to be seen. Take your time and sit with this last sentence.

You don't like the way you dance, so you don't go to the school dance. But to get rid of the shame, you have to meet yourself with compassion and allow yourself to dance, especially because you have a longing to go dancing. In fact, you have no proof that you are the worst dancer or that someone else is the best. Comparing yourself with another person is a shaming tactic as well. There's no reason for you to compare your dance skills. (Replace *dance* with any aspect at different points in your life.)

There's no reason for you to compare your skills, talents, and what you can do based on the next person. That's a game that no human will ever win, which is why it's not worth playing. Playing that game takes you out of the richness of your experience and blocks you from showing up.

In the context of the dance, go and get a nice shirt or dress that you like. Get some shoes that inspire you, that make you feel good. Express yourself through your clothing not because you need to be liked or approved but because the outfit reflects what you feel inside. Dance when a song comes on that you love, and if a full-blown routine feels odd for you, start small and move your shoulders or bob your head. Allow your body to connect to the present, to the sounds, to the bass vibrations. When an unfamiliar one comes on, dance to that. Allow your body to bounce to the rhythm.

What is the point of holding it in? Oh, that's right, because shame-bound people don't express openly—unless they drink alcohol, I presume. But is that freedom? No. Because of shame, you develop addictions to help you escape the shame. The real solution, the one that offers longevity and true transformation, is to allow yourself to be seen. You can do this without alcohol—you can do this sober. You can.

And for you, your thread might not be dancing but the dance analogy can apply to all of our lives. Switch the narrative to fit your life. See yourself as the person who has the courage to compassionately face his or her shame wounds, and please use kindness towards yourself as you abolish old wounds and old stories.

Here's a list of a person who is on the other side of that, and when you read this list, I hope you realize that these are available to you as well. This transformation is available to you as soon as you decide to stop isolating. The second that you bring in a community and allow yourself to be seen, the energy starts to change, that is how we begin to accept and gawk at the richness of life.

Mood Board for the Person Who Allows Themselves to Be Seen (Shame Does Not Rule Here)

"I am here for the world."
"The world is here for me."
"I accept me for who I am."
"I am grateful for who I am today."
"I'm a human, and I don't have to be perfect."
"I have never done that, but I'm willing to try."
"I have not mastered this. I am curious about it."
"My relationships with my family are being healed."
"No matter what, I learn, I try, and I have fun in life."
"I am worthy of relationships that have love and trust."
"My family and I respect that we have different voices."
"I'm not good at this, so I want to learn what I can to get better."
"I trust my ability to discern who is good for me and who is not."
"I am different from my family, and that is okay. I am able to find things that I love about them while accepting myself fully."

Three Focuses to Recognize on Healing Shame

Have a safe conversation about your shame. Shame is an emotions that we outcast and try not to make space for. What happens when we allow shame to sit at the table with all the other emotions? What happens when we make a safe space for it? Shame is meant to be witnessed, and once it's seen, a level of freedom and healing will find you.

When the shame is covered and a secret, it becomes hard to process, hard to deal with. Trust that whatever you are ashamed about, you are not alone.

There is help, there's support, and someone in your community is most likely dealing with the same thing. It's hard, but you have to allow yourself to open up so the shame can breathe. Once your shame gets fresh air, it doesn't smell as potent as before.

Talk kindlier to yourself. Shame is what tells you to call yourself an idiot, moron, or stupid. Shame is what tells you that you're not good enough or that you'll never be enough. The presence of shame changes our relationship with language and nothing is more important than how use words to tell our stories.

Shame is a nemesis, and one of the best ways to attack it is to choose loving language. You have to speak to yourself in kinder ways; every time you do, you ask shame to leave your soul. The way we get rid of shame is to use love and empathy. Shame cannot grow in places where love and empathy are present.

Learn to touch more. When shame runs through you, touch may not exist — especially if you grew up in a shame-bound household where healthy touch was outcast. Touch is important because it helps you with intimacy, it helps you feel like you belong, and it brings people closer. Safe touch has the ability to heal the nervous system.

Where there is intimacy and trust, shame cannot live. Use touch every single day as you become more aligned with yourself, and with those around you.

I hope you choose to practice loving kindness and lean into healthy coping skills. True healing, genuine love and higher vibrations are available to you at every moment.

—Sylvester McNutt III • Loving Kindness

When you feel the emotion of shame coming over your soul, speak about it and please be kind to yourself when you do so. Do not allow it to weigh on you. Take a step back, breathe, and speak what you are feeling. This practice will help the shame feel smaller and smaller as your practice gets stronger and bigger. Be proud of yourself for the courage it takes to do this every single time.

—Sylvester McNutt III • Courage

If you see an adult that you know shaming a child, pull them aside and make them aware of what they're doing. They may not be aware, and if you feel the shame inside you as you see it, you owe it to that child to give them what you want someone to do for you.

—Sylvester McNutt III • Stand Tall

When friends and family bring to you their problems, please understand that you do not have to attach yourself to their problems. Have boundaries with what you take on. There's a difference between looking at a pair of shoes and wearing them. You don't have to wear their shoes; choose wisely with what you take on, how much, and for how long.

— Sylvester McNutt III • Boundaries

If you have to set boundaries, one of the best phrases you can use is "No, I do not accept that." Another one is "I cannot help you." Having clear boundaries helps you be honest to your capabilities and limits. Having boundaries is all about self-love and self-respect.

—Sylvester McNutt III • Boundaries

If you were shamed in a previous relationship, it may be hard to be yourself fully today. I challenge you to surround yourself with the people who actually want you to be who you are; you know who those people are. They have an energy that feels different, and yes, that's because they just want to be loved like you do. Be around people who want you to be your truest self — that's self-love.

—Sylvester McNutt III • That's Self-Love

When you feel the emotion of shame coming over your soul, ask yourself, "Do I have to hold these thoughts?" and "Are these my words, or am I repeating the words of someone who no longer matters to my story?" And sometimes this little practice allows you to let go of thoughts that you don't own and that have no business being in your presence today. You are free from thoughts that do not align with you, your destiny or your healing practice — release them.

—Sylvester McNutt III • You Are Free

If you isolate all the time, I want you to ask, "Am I isolating because the people around me are dangerous?" If so, recognize that you need new people in your life. We are meant to get solitude from time to time, but isolation is different. Isolation is running away from love, community, and intimacy. We are meant to be in community so please, go get new people who make you feel loved and safe.

—Sylvester McNutt III • Get New People

4

Respect Your Hands: Letting Go Of Unruly Thoughts And Emotions

IF YOU LOOK DOWN AT YOUR HANDS, YOU'LL SEE RIDGES, indentations, and patterns. You could reach out right now and squeeze, grab, and pull something tangible. The beautiful thing about hands is that they help you move, fight, and love. They help us draw, paint and balance. They help us bathe, eat and defend ourselves.

They enable you to swim, cartwheel, and climb a tree if need be. Some of us do not have a full set of fingers; some of us have burns and birthmarks on our hands. Some of our hands are weak and fragile, some are strong and sturdy.

When we reach deep into the toolbox of healing, of peace of mind, of moving on into higher vibrations, we must imagine trying to run a mile while holding a twenty-five-pound plate in both hands while wearing a weighted vest —what will that feel like? Is it possible? Yes, of course, it is very possible to run a mile like that. However, I wonder if we could, at the very least, let go of the plates that we are holding in our hand, even if the resistance will still be on our shoulders and back. I wonder what is available to us right now in the present. I wonder what we could let go of or at least begin to practice to let go of right now.

Beginning the Practice of Letting Go

Language is important, and the language of letting go may set us up for failure if we are not fully conscious of our expectation as we use the phrase. Over the years, I've learned a few language tips that have helped me reframe my attempts at letting go. I'll explain those here as we begin to unpack the "how to let go" question.

When you hear the words *letting go*, what you may be expecting is ***forget it happened*** or ***totally get rid of that one thing***. And what may help you is changing the expectation of the language to something softer and more subtle like ***learning a new behavior to fall back on when that situation happens*** or ***becoming aware of my reactions so I can choose a new one***.

Another element of letting go is often time. You've heard famous phrases like "Time heals all wounds" or "Healing takes time," and I wonder if it is possible that healing or letting go doesn't exist on the axis of time but instead on that of presence, attention and language. Of course, one will argue that presence is time, but is it really? Is it possible that we don't need time to heal but instead a realistic practice, attention to what's available to us in the moment, and the power to understand the words that we are using and how we are associating with them? Is it possible, by bringing this to our awareness, that we can begin to let go immediately—right now? Is that possible?

How do you let go of a strong emotion?

You ask yourself, "Is this mine to hold at this moment?" Another question that I love is, what version of me is showing up in this situation? Most of the time, you'll see that what's around you doesn't even belong to you; and other times, you'll see that it's not the adult version of you that is showing up. Instead, it may be the child in you, the one who has a painful wound that hasn't been processed or acknowledged.

You'll begin to feel a deep connection with the present as well when you ask, "Which me is showing up, and is this mine to hold?" Why is that? I believe it's because you offer yourself the gift of compassion, and you allow yourself to slow down and become totally present.

Letting go is essential in saying, "I choose to give myself compassion as an option as I process what is happening or what happened." Letting go means making sacred space for ourselves and others; it means coming into an agreement of acceptance with the past. And that enables the process of grieving, seeing it authentically, observing it fully, and finally saying, "I am letting go of this hook that has been lodged in my soul." Some stages may take longer than others, but that is okay as long as we remind ourselves to come back to the present.

I have a hard time letting go of emotions when I am emotional. Sometimes I get into it with my partner, and because I am emotional, it just becomes too much. What should I do?

Be kind to yourself; don't look at your reactions as if you are defective. It's possible that the patterns and reactions you are used implementing are ineffective methods of communication, that may be very true. But don't interpret that as *I am a defective person.* It could be that you are protecting yourself, and so you become overwhelmed and you are using this pattern as a defense mechanism. You and your partner must recognize that our work here is to try to make the environment safe for both of you. It's not about blame, critique, or trying to be right—this is about creating a safe space for each one of you to ease into the conflict.

You have to create a safe container for how you process emotions, and you also should become one with your breath when those moments arise. I'm willing to bet that you do not have a practice for how you process emotions. For example, when hot and heavy emotions arise, do you have a practice that helps you acknowledge them? Do you have a routine that helps you safely deal with what you experience, or do you allow the triggers of each moment to take hold? As a practical tool you should implement a daily meditation practice for the purpose of connecting with your breath, slowing down and balancing your energy.

The very first step you can take when strong emotions arise is to take a breath. If you pause for a few seconds and deeply inhale and exhale, you'll begin to enter the present, and then you can ask yourself, "What is going on here?"

I used to deal with anger issues as a teenager; it

wasn't until I got to college that I learned how to breathe more effectively from one of the soccer players at my college. I used to run four to five miles with her a few times during the week. For her, five miles was nothing, and I asked her the secret. She said, "The more you run, the better your lungs get."

The more you breathe, pause, and gather what's happening, the easier it becomes to process any emotional spark. Previously your problem is that you never had a system to check-in with yourself, and now you do. The next time something arises, try to find your breath and breathe.

What if my partner, parents, or friends do not understand how I need to process and let go of things?

It's not your job to convince or persuade them to understand; it's only your job to share with them the inner workings of the process so they may understand. You don't need their approval for how you need to heal but it is your duty to share how or what you need. For example, in my life, I need time to myself to decompress after strong energetic exchanges. I am clear and direct when I feel this need arise.

At this point, you want to introduce language that slows the conversation down. As a former sports guy, I love saying things like "Hey, I'm hearing what you are saying, and I'm trying to understand. However, we need to take a time-out because there are some things I missed. Also, I have a few key points I want to go over again." Or " I want to make sure you understand how I process things, especially when I get angry, or I don't feel heard. Here's how I process things. Here's *how* my brain works. Do you understand?" Doing this will create an invitation into how you communicate, which creates that space for understanding. The key is to create more compassion for yourself and those around you.

What do I do when the conversation moves so fast that I can't even figure out what I'm thinking?

Oftentimes, we cannot process what is happening when we are talking to someone because the conversation keeps moving, and we keep making connections with what is being said. And that time needed to process and acknowledge something comes and goes because there are so many topics to cover.

When this happens, we have to set a clear intention with this conversation and with our time. Sometimes we simply need to stop and go back. Sometimes we need to stop, think, and feel that moment. We are not taught that taking a time-out or a pause is okay. I will argue that more relationships will ease conflict if both parties bring this framework in—simply pause, take a break, and go back or sit still together so both can get up to speed. The language that works well in this situation is "I'm loving the energy and passion we have in this conversation. However, I think our pace is too fast. Let's set the intention to slow down and take our time with this. How does that sound for you?"

I miss my ex — How do I let go of that feeling?

Getting rid of that feeling may not be the right target; instead, what we could do is begin to focus on honoring what the relationship was. There is nothing wrong with reminiscing, missing, and thinking about good times. But for our present moment, it is vital that we do not continue to carry emotional baggage that no longer serves this present journey. When we think of an ex, wish them well. Also, I wonder, did you ever grieve this ending in the presence of a community? If not, it's time to grieve, respectfully.

I was doing a workshop one time, and someone said, "Well, I don't wish anything bad to happen to them."

And I said, "Yes, but you're not wishing them well. There's a big energetic difference there." You're choosing to feel like they are unworthy of the best treatment, and maybe that connects to some residue or unresolved pain that you have never processed.

Yes, I understand that all relationships have pain points, and it may be hard to wish someone well who hurt you; I accept that. But I care about your healing, and for your healing, the last thing you need to do is restrict yourself from wishing them well.

It's a slight vibrational difference, but it can feel

like freedom. Wish them well, wish them love, wish for them to get all the love. As you begin to think of them, your future thoughts will become simply *I wish them well*, and then you will move on from that thought easier without bringing any baggage into the moment. This takes time; be patient. Wish them well, but also, wish yourself well too.

I tried to let go a million times and it doesn't work, what should I do?

Answer these questions:

1. Is that thing that you are holding on to yours to hold?

2. What will happen if you choose to let go?

3. What are you afraid of? Is this fear as potent as you perceive it be or have you manifested more fear by constantly projecting what may or may not happen?

4. Have you brought in a village of people on this thing, or are you'd doing it alone? If you are doing it alone, it will be tough and could be damn near impossible. You must allow these moments to be seen and witnessed by others. It's time to talk with a counselor, teacher, therapist, your spouse, or your friends. The days of doing things alone are over.

5. What would happen if you said, "I release this and I am allowing it to fade away?"

How to Stay Engaged When Trying to Let Go of a Tough Time or Strong Emotions

1. ***Stay engaged in your movement.*** I respect that we all have different forms of movements we love. When you are going through it, do not skip your weights, your walks, or your stretches because that four to eight percent of your day is going to give you positive emotions that will help you heal. It's going to keep your mind off what is bothering you, and it gives you a safe space to still touch base with the most powerful emotion—love.

2. ***Recommit to sleeping and eating well.*** When we go through a hard time, we may choose behaviors that don't help us, like staying up all night eating Cheetos or a whole bag of cookies and drinking beer excessively. There's a time and place for everything, and when we are going through a tough time, we have to be conscious of our sleep and what we're eating.

   Recommit to sleeping at least eight hours per night; science has shown us that we need sleep. Going to bed on time will help us with those late-night munchies as well. Go to bed and wake up at the same time (develop this habit, it will only reward you). If you are serious about self-love then go to bed and get the rest you deserve. Also, if you have kids, I know first hand how challenging it can be to get some sleep. If you find yourself not getting the sleep you need because of young children, then please try your best to reduce your stress during your waking hours.

3. ***Don't do this alone; open up.*** If you feel like you are going through a hard time, bring in the people you share your life with. With respect to your situation, share what you feel comfortable with. Tell people exactly how they can support you on this mission. Do this no matter what team you are on. Most people want to help, most people want to go all out, and most people will help you if you are honest. Be yourself—even your *I'm going through something right now* self—and people will show up for you every single time.

With all due respect,
let go of what you need
to let go of so new energy
and possibility can flow
into your life.
—Sylvester McNutt III • Self-Love

Sometimes letting go is the wrong target. There are some things we never let go of. Instead, we must learn how to cope, how to manage, and how to gain the right perspective so we can live with peace of mind and calmness. Moving on may not happen, but peace of mind and acceptance of what is will always available to us. Allow yourself to process what you are going through and don't rush yourself to let go of it. You'll get there; give yourself self-compassion when attempting to let go.

Sylvester McNutt III • Self-Compassion

To move forward with new energy and a new way of seeing the world, you have to look at the old behaviors that you're repeating over and over — and you must choose to release them. Your transformation lives on the other side of those behaviors and outdated mindsets.

Tell yourself: ***I am letting go of the behaviors that keep me from my highest vibration.*** I will operate from the highest vibration: love.

-Sylvester McNutt III • Let Go Of The Old You

MOVING INTO PEACE OF MIND

Moving on might be the wrong target today. Words matter, and when people mention moving on, often they mean never thinking of a situation again, and that might be the wrong target for us. Let's allow ourselves to focus on gaining a new perspective, a new feeling and association when sensory images trigger us.

After a breakup, hearing your ex's favorite artist may bring anger. After a while, though, that artist can bring closure. You can begin to say things like "This is a great song, and I'm thankful I learned from that relationship." Doing that has to be genuine, and when it is, it brings you healing and changes your association with the triggers.

Journal when you are going through it. In times of high emotional energy it's important that you process those emotions. Getting your thoughts, ideas, and emotions out on paper helps you cope and process them. One of the best tactics to move on from emotions are to reconnect with your breath and to write them down. To write what you're feeling or seeing can greatly aid your ability to process.

What can you control? I ask myself this question every single day, especially when I see someone acting a certain way that does not align with my vibrations. The more you ask yourself this question, the more you point your power inward.

Most people give away their power, neglect their power, and choose to not step into the moment. Bring yourself to the present and ask, "What can I control?" Begin to move from your power, and you'll have more peace of mind. If you allow everyone to trigger you, to bother you, to get to you, then you will always suffer. Recognizing and releasing what you do not have control over brings you into a place of peace of mind.

Make your choice wisely.

We do not talk enough about grieving and how potent of a process it is. I hope you allow yourself to grieve all of the endings that you have experienced. You have all the permission needed to properly grieve any loss or change.

—Sylvester McNutt III • Grieve

One of the most beautiful processes we have as human beings is the ability to grieve. In the context of loving yourself properly, give yourself the compassion to respect and honor your grieving process. You do not have to fake getting over something just for fake peace of mind. True healing comes only when you respect yourself, when you forgive yourself and when you use self-compassion, daily.

—Sylvester McNutt III • You Are Healing

We have to learn how to
embrace endings. Everything
in life is forever changing and
shifting. Learning how to let
go means learning how to live.

—Sylvester McNutt III

Self-love is allowing yourself to grieve. Self-love is honoring the endings and cherishing the emotions that come with endings.

—Sylvester McNutt III

We need to throw away the idea that endings need to be painful, draining, and one-sided. We are allowed to be thankful, grateful while also making space for sorrow and discomfort. Learning how to do endings shows us how to live fully, how to live in a room of deep appreciation.

—Sylvester McNutt III

When I think about this society, I often wonder: what would it be like if we had grief rituals, if grieving was an ordinary conversation, and if we all took time to learn how to witness friends and family grieve. Where would we be if we leaned into grieving properly without preaching to people to *just let it go.*

—Sylvester McNutt III

When you are not operating at your highest frequency, do not fake your good vibes and your positivity. Sit with what you are going through, honor it, and allow your body to process it. You will be okay because you are designed to cope; you regenerate and you heal, naturally. You are not designed to ignore the real just so you can fake the funk for them. Give yourself permission to be authentic.

—Sylvester McNutt III • You Are Healing

Throw away the idea that you have to be okay and that you have to have it all figured out. Let's move on from that idea, and let's embrace that life is a journey of love, questions, and experiences. And when you are not okay, do not fight that alone. Bring your energy into a community; bring your sorrow and pain into a safe vessel so it can be met properly. Self-love is about bringing your pain to the forefront so you can see it, so space can be made for it.

—Sylvester McNutt III • You Are Healing

Ask yourself and be honest, **"Is this mine to hold?"** At least ninety percent or more of what you're holding on to does not belong to this *present* version of you. This present version of you deserves to be free. Let it go; you deserve to get the weight off you. Release the residue of yesterday — you are free today.

If you are struggling with moving on, always remember that low points happen to all of us. When you get in a point that feels low, don't pile on and beat yourself up. Honor that moment and allow yourself to be there. There's no reason to rush your healing process; it's best to learn who you are now and to honor each phase of transition, even the parts you want to push past.

—Sylvester McNutt III • You Are Healing

One of the biggest life hacks on moving on from a toxic person or even a version of yourself that you no longer want to be is to ***create new habits that nourish your soul.*** Doing this creates new soil, and those old plants can live in this new earth.

—Sylvester McNutt III • You Are Healing

Accept the situation for what it is. The sooner you allow yourself to do this, the quicker you move on. Freedom is waiting for you on the other side of acceptance. Be free!

—Sylvester McNutt III • Acceptance

Moving on is about choosing not to live in the past. You can't go back and change anything, so bring your thoughts to the present. What can you do in this moment? That's where your attention and effort should go — this moment only.

—Sylvester McNutt III • Presence

Allow yourself to be free from repeating stories over and over that do not serve you. These stories do nothing but bring you into a lower vibration and they support the mindsets and patterns that you don't want. They bringup the old emotions and trap you in a pattern. Respectfully, stop repeating those stories. Be mindful of the stories you tell yourself and others.

—Sylvester McNutt III • Mindful Of Your Words

Be mindful of the words and stories you use to describe your life. Words have the ability to encourage, inspire and heal you if used right. Use words and stories that lift you into your highest self.

—Sylvester McNutt III • Mindful Of Your Words

Throw away the idea that moving on means moving to something better or worse. Sometimes the focus just needs to be *I have to get out of this space. What comes next will come once I clear the energy of the now.*

Growth is not always about better, more, or bolder. Sometimes growth is as simple as letting go of what no longer aligns with your life so you can be your healthiest self. You don't have to know what the next move is to know that it's time to release this present one.

Be free...

— Sylvester McNutt III

Any person who consistently lets you down or brings you down is someone you must build healthy boundaries with, and if that's not possible, then you should consider letting them take their energy elsewhere. You are not responsible for their behavior, but you are responsible for what you allow, for what you choose, and for who you allow into your life.

—Sylvester McNutt III • Boundaries

Detachment is a tool. Use it when healing and self-love is the focus. Some things and people do not deserve to be attached to your soul, and some do. ***Choose wisely.***

Detachment is a tool that can help you if you allow it. Letting go of what no longer serves you brings greater purpose, clarity, and understanding into your life. Let go so you can vibrate higher.

-- Sylvester McNutt III

We had a dark past, but we always knew we deserved a bright future. That is why the present is so vital for people like us because it balances all our thoughts. Thinking of the past can bring pain and can hold us back. Seeing the future brings love, excitement, and joy. It's beautiful that we have the present because there is love, healing, and clarity here.

—Sylvester McNutt III • Bright Future

When you make intense choices that result in letting go of jobs, people, and situations that don't flow with your life anymore, alchemy happens. The act of letting go welcomes space for new people, places, and experiences that you would not have attracted if you held on.

—Sylvester McNutt III • Letting Go

Sometimes you have two options: go back and fix what you can or move forward and learn from the times. Listen to your body; it's communicating with you. You know what is possible. Don't ignore yourself because you have the answer deep down inside. It will work if that is what you want, but if it's time to go away, be gone.

—Sylvester McNutt III • Listen

Stop doing things you hate.
Choose-self love.
Stop doing things you hate.
Choose-self love.
Stop doing things you hate.
Choose-self love.
Stop doing things you hate.
Choose-self love.
Stop doing things you hate.
Choose-self love.
Stop doing things you hate.
Choose-self love.
Stop doing things you hate.
Choose-self love.

Stop doing things you hate. Choose self-love. If you let go of what you hate and low vibrational emotions that live inside you, you'll make more space for abundance, love, peace of mind, and the life that you deserve. Stop doing what you hate and spend your energy on love. Spend time on your passions, things that excite you and light you up!

— Sylvester McNutt III • Listen

Sometimes we are obsessed with not letting go because we need to know what's next — we love the allusion of certainty. If you are here, then embrace mystery; embrace not knowing. There's so much beauty and love in the *I don't know* areas of life. There's so much to learn about the unknown, the unseen, the untouched. Open your heart to these spaces even if there's fear present.

—Sylvester McNutt III • Embrace The Unknown

Moving on is not always easy because sometimes we don't know what we are moving on to, and we love certainty. The truth is we don't know what's going to happen next, and our focus should not be on what's next; it needs to be on the now. We need presence and healing, and attention to our wounds in this moment. That is self-love and true healing. Your next phase will come — it always does, until then, put all of your attention on the now.

—Sylvester McNutt III • The Now

Moving on is available to you today, but you have to become totally present to move on. You can't skip this moment of your life. Moving on doesn't work when you say, "I want to go from my past to my future." You are skipping the most important part—the now. Allow yourself to fall in love with the clouds of today, the water that will enter your body today, and the air that flows through your lungs in this moment.

—Sylvester McNutt III • Embrace The Unknown

To go to your next level, let go of the parts of your mindset that hold you back. Ask, "Do I have to hold on to this thought, or can I let it go for a thought that is going to serve me compassionately?"

Sylvester McNutt III • Embrace The Unknown

I no longer like the word *failure* when describing our journeys. It's hard to let go of something if we see ourselves as a failure (which brings us shame); instead, let's begin to talk with more compassion and love to ourselves. We may have failed at a moment, but we are not a failure as a human — we are allowed to grow and evolve.
—Sylvester McNutt III

I never focus on how another person treats me—never. I focus on what I am willing to accept, what I will allow, and what type of energy is welcomed in my life. I focus on what I want, replenishing my energy and exactly how my exceptional life is going to flow. I focus on communicating my wants and needs and allowing the right people to seamlessly fit into my life. I attract what I want, and what is not for me will naturally let go of me. I am assertive for the life that I deserve. This is the art of alignment.

Sylvester McNutt III

I do not focus on trying to change my past; instead, I honor everything I went through and all the people I've met. And my promise to myself is that I will stay present and focused on my passions, purpose and healing. I will treat myself with compassion and let go of whatever I am not meant to hold.

— Sylvester McNutt III

My hands are strong, but they cannot hold everything. My heart is strong, but it does not beat for everybody. My back is strong, but I cannot carry everyone forever. I'll give when I can, help when I can, but I have boundaries, and those require me to always treat myself with compassion. And that means saying no when I don't have it to give. I'll do my best for the next person, but self-love is accepting and acknowledging my own limits.

—Sylvester McNutt III

Endings are a normal part of living, and you do not have to find silver linings or fake positivity. Self-love is about being honest and authentic with the story you are telling. It's allowed to suck, to be the bottom, to be awful. You do not have to rush to change the narrative, and you do not have to find the good in it, either. Compassionately, please understand that all things can be healed, yes, but you're allowed to be one hundred percent authentic with how you feel in this moment. Doing so is how you authentically heal and process your grief. You're allowed to feel what you feel.

—Sylvester McNutt III

5

FIRE YOUR PERFORMER: TAPPING INTO YOUR HIGHEST SELF

THIS CHAPTER IS A WARM LOOK AT HOW TO LET GO of people-pleasing and perfection without shame.

This is an invitation to operate from the authentic energy that is inside you while breaking up with the behaviors that keep you trapped in people-pleasing and chasing perfection just to be liked.

Are you tired of not revealing your feelings aloud? Are you tired of setting a muzzle on your mouth because you're *too loud*, or you don't *say the right thing*? Are you tired of pretending to agree so your family can accept whatever version of you they want you to be? Don't you get tired of using your professional voice, saving face, and lying to yourself to keep a minimum wage opportunity? Do you get tired of concealing your dream because your parents will never get it and all they want to do is push to you what they think is best while never asking you who you are or what you want? I bet you are.

From an energy perspective, that act sounds draining; and when it comes to self-love, the most critical point of awareness is to ask, "How am I using my energy each day? Am I using it in an authentic and fulfilling way, or am I lying to myself and hiding to get by."

If you are nodding and saying, "Yes, it's time for a change," then it's time to fire your performer. That performer that continues to show up to the party does not help you, friend, and I say this with compassion. That people-pleasing son of a bitch that you fall back on, at some point, may have offered you safety from a real threat. But at this moment, you have to recognize that he or she is nothing more than a threat to your soul, to the richness of your connection, to your ability to show up in the world in a way that makes you fulfilled and authentic.

If our game here is to learn how to love ourselves properly, then that means we no longer have time for perfection or people-pleasing. It means the performer has to be taken off life support, for they are taking the energy, resources, and attention that we need to resurrect the life that we deserve. Once we let this performer go, we will indeed be able to hold on to our most genuine and authentic life, and that opportunity is available to us in this moment.

SET THE SCENE

Imagine you are a fly on the wall, and you're watching Vanessa Morales backstage in the makeup chair before going out in front of the crowd to do a new show. She's going over her lines repeatedly, rehearsing her reactions and words. She's mentally preparing to get into the character of Grace Alexandria, the singing, dancing, flipping, magic-trick-doing performer whom people travel across the world to see. Grace is promoted as a passionate and successful Venezuelan woman.

The real human behind the character Grace, Vanessa, puts all her emotions, ideas, and thoughts to the side because she is about to entertain an audience of 2,500. She completely abandons her principles, morals, and ideas because nobody has paid to see her—we all are paying to see her performance, which in this context is totally acceptable, right?

But my question to you is this: when we, in our real lives, abandon who we are and we put all our emotions, ideas, and thoughts to the side just so we can entertain or be accepted by whoever, who are we choosing to be? Isn't this how we get trapped in these people-pleasing cycles? Isn't this how we get trapped in cycles that don't help us produce the life we love? So the question becomes, what practices must we do or what belief systems should we tap into to free ourselves from the cycle? Our work here is to learn how to break up with people-pleasing. The only time we should see performing arts is when we go to the theatre or when we turn on the television.

Let Go Of People-Pleasing And Do This:

Become more present.
Be a place of welcome.
Spend time being yourself.
Be honest about what you want.
Spend more time on your passion.
Practice using your authentic voice.
Practice detachment from others' opinions.

Breaking Up with People-Pleasing and Performing Just to Be Liked

1. ***Spend time being yourself.*** This is about accepting that your work in the moment means spending more time with people who allow you to be yourself; it means spending more energy on events and activities that allow you to be yourself. And if you don't know what being yourself genuinely means, then that's wonderful because now you have an invitation to explore what that means for your life.

2. ***Practice detachment from others' opinions.*** As you blossom into your deepest vibration, you'll recognize that other people's opinion of you does not have to alter, shift, or change how you are. It's really just a thought—one that does not have to matter.

3. ***Become more present.*** Often the desire to be liked is a future desire. *If I do this behavior, then their response will be approval of me.* Come to the present moment with an affirmation and an intention to connect to your breath, to your body. This will help you battle those thoughts about the future.

4. ***Spend more time on your passion.*** If you are worried about what others are saying, then you are not spending enough time on your passions. When you get

locked in to your passions, it can be so magnetic that it pulls in all your focus.

5. *Be a place of welcome.* This one is not as obvious because we are not used to thinking this way. What we want is often what we need to create. We get into this *I want the world to serve me* mindset, but the truth is we need to *begin to serve ourselves and others*. As we become a place of welcome, more love, abundance, harmony, and peace of mind come in.

Throw Away the Idea That You Need to Perform to Be Liked

The act is killing your happiness, your energy, your power; the ability to be your most genuine self is what is going to give you the alignment you deserve. Aligning mind, body and soul is the goal here. The *I need to perform* stance is killing your ability to be seen and held as you are—but that starts with you. It keeps you away from creativity, expression, and the richness of life. The act is keeping you away from healing, from growing your body and soul. Constantly performing is keeping you bound to the trauma that is deeply woven into the act.

Performing for the sake of satiating other people's desires of who you are and who you have to be is exhausting. Performing for Mom and Dad doesn't fill them up and nourish them; it only appeases them, and it leaves you starving for more. How much longer are you going to appease others while leaving yourself dull and fighting for the scraps of life?

Performing is draining; it's useless. You keep yourself in a bind when you perform to appease others daily. The bind is a sacrifice of self, also known as self-betrayal. "I am going to help them and hurt myself." How much longer will you allow this to go on? Does this inspire your potency, or does it make you weaker? Is this choice a choice that is less than love — if so, how much longer can we continue to choose it? Please, throw away the idea that you need to perform to be liked.

It's essential for your potency that you allow yourself to cook the part of yourself that feels the need to perform for everyone in your life. The part of you that says, "I need to perform," needs to be brought into the *nigredo*, and you have to process that material. You have to face this part of you, and you have to hold yourself, so let's talk about another way of *how* you can do this.

On the following, you'll see my nine-step program for diving deeper into your most authentic self. Use this list not as an end-all suggestion but more as a starting point that can ignite the energy to breakup with the need to perform. When implementing this list be sure to use the upmost compassion and love for yourself.

How to Stop Performing so You Can Be Your Authentic Self

- Play every single day.
- Be okay with impermanence.
- Stop chasing goals that aren't yours.
- Allow yourself to express what you feel.
- Don't pressure yourself to be in the future.
- Heal in a community and stop doing it alone.
- Do spend more time in places that feel like home.
- Don't go with the flow if that's not what you want.
- Accept that you do not need to have it all together.

Play every single day

Have fun with yourself. Do you allow yourself to have fun, to laugh, to play, or are you focusing on paying bills and stress? I wonder what life would be like for many of us if we allowed in more play and fun.

When you are caught up in the future—what you should be doing and what you could do—all you do is ripen the seeds of worry and anxiety. Allow yourself to play more in the present.

It seems like growing up is about growing out of play, yet so many adults search for opportunities to play because those moments make us feel alive. So my question is, what is the purpose of giving up playing if it's going to be something we forever seek?

Give yourself permission to have fun, learn, dance, sing, stretch, and use your imagination. There is no reason to be serious and stressed. Why? Who is selling us the dream that we need to chase stress? That is a sale that I need a refund for because it didn't work for me.

I believe that there are some things we should take seriously, like our boundaries and our health. I challenge you to reflect on the things you take seriously and ask, "If I substituted some of those activities or focal points with play, how would I feel? Would there be a shift in my life, a change that would affect my community in a light that felt good?"

Be okay with impermanence

What stays the same in life? Would you agree that everything changes in life? Most people would agree with that statement — don't you? Okay, so if you believe everything changes, then why do you keep the performer in you who has lived in you for as long as you can remember? As a kid, yes, you empowered that performer because you wanted him or her to be safe. In most cases, the performer exists so you can satisfy a need for safety. But at this point, you are no longer a child.

You are grown, and you may even have a child or aspire to be a parent one day. Let me ask, do you want your kid to perform for you? Or do you want your kid to live his or her life fully and do what makes him or her the happiest and healthiest?

Why is it that we all want our kids to be as happiest as they can be, but we aren't willing to give that to ourselves? Do we not realize that the children are watching us? Please give yourself the permission that you are attempting to give your kids. You deserve that too.

My favorite term right now is evolution. Evolution may be described as any net directional change or any collective change in the properties of organisms or populations over many generations. Evolution is the biological development of a species over some time. The process of evolution keeps a species alive and thriving and allows organisms to pass down their genes successfully. Here are some of the most obvious things that have evolved in our lifetime:

- Technology
- Social Media
- Electric Cars
- Video games
- The meat industry
- Moth's darker wings
- Information on nutrition
- Race relations in the United States
- Information on how to heal the body
- The rise of added sugar and fast food
- The rise of the millionaire population

We are meant to evolve, to grow, to shed, to grieve, to become new. We are meant to live and die, and to ask a bunch of questions along the way. As we evolve, let's be kind to ourselves and practice being okay with change. The better we are with change, the easier life's frictions points feel — and that feels like self-love to me. Embrace evolution and lean deeply into your role and participation in your development.

STOP CHASING GOALS THAT AREN'T YOURS

The most disrespectful thing you can do is chase goals that are not true to you. Why are you pursuing what you think is going to make Mom and Dad happy? If you love what you are pursuing, then by all means, dive in. The most respectful thing you can do is honor your life and your path.

As children, we want approval from our parents; but as we get older and become potent adults ourselves, we have to do away with our childish ways. We must grow our bodies, souls, and experience, and it's possible that our parents will not like or love every choice we make. But our mission here is not to appease anymore. We are here to show up fully and love ourselves properly, which means our goals may not align with what they feel is best.

As a parent myself, I trust how I am raising my kid, and I trust that he will make sound decisions through years of me being there for him as he figures out what's best for him. Also, he will make poor decisions due to a lack of experience, and he will do things that I may not like or agree with. His work is to recognize that he is not living for me, he is living for him. My work is to recognize that my role is to support him and not to control him (I hope you realize this for you, as well).

But at some point, I have to pull back, and I have to empower him to be his potent version. At some point, I have to say, "Okay, you have the juice. Go for it and see what happens." If you are an adult dealing with this, let your parents know that you have the juice now and that you must be allowed the space to make your own decisions.

If you too are a parent, pull back and trust your kid who is now an adult. Empower him or her with trust and support, coming from a space where there is no shame or judgment. We need each other; we need to be seen in a community as we find our voice.

ALLOW YOURSELF TO EXPRESS WHAT YOU FEEL

The performer doesn't give a damn about you. The performer only wants to protect him-or herself to live deep inside you. That's why you lie about how you feel, and that is why you don't lean into your feelings—because the performer will not allow you.

Today you are taking your power back. Fire your performer so you can lean into how you feel. As a man, I know this all too well. We men don't lean into our emotions because it can be viewed as weak, which is an extreme mindset. I will argue that it's even more insane and extreme to deny ourselves of our humanity, which is to emote.

And as a former athlete, a current video game nerd, and a father, I can say that men do emote all the time. It's just not in the vessel that women are allowed to. You see how turned up a man gets when his team loses or when his character dies in *Call of Duty*. (This is me projecting right now, but it's okay — I have no shame, ha.) And any father can tell you that kids trigger emotions in you that you didn't even know existed: pure joy, immense fulfillment and the curiosity of why the house is sticky!

So to any man reading this, not acknowledging and making space for your emotions is a lie because you do it in the vessel of sports and with your children. I want to invite you to tap into other vessels and other emotions that may not feel safe because those repressed emotions are nothing but cages. You can still be manly, tough, and a leader if that is what you desire. It's okay to say, "I feel this way" or "I feel that way." It's human. And this goes for everyone. Please, free yourself from your emotions and allow them to pass. Some of them need to be spoken on, written about, or emoted to safely pass them.

Don't pressure yourself to be in the future

I do not plan seventy years or seven years or seven months into the future. The longer you live, the more you see that too much can happen quickly over extended periods. I plan twelve weeks at a time—at most, because I run a business, have a child and I love to travel. That helps me with the practical nature of running my business, the ever-changing landscape of being a parent, and the always shifting space of being human.

I've tried yearly goals and all the things that are often recommended to us, and for me, none of it feels like home. Breaking the year into quarters and going twelve weeks at a time give me the most momentum to push for goals, but it does not give so much pressure that my mental health is in ruins. I encourage you to look at your life, and when it comes to a planning perspective, a goal perspective, figure out what makes you feel the most comfortable.

I could rattle off goals that do exist in the three-to seven-year time frame, but they're loose and not rigid. The purpose of the twelve-week plan is to be tighter, be intentional, and lead you into your big goals. I look at the twelve-week plan as a small step. A bunch of small steps is how we eventually get to where we want to go. Small steps are required even in big goals.

HEAL IN A COMMUNITY AND STOP DOING IT ALONE

I have to admit that I did this for far too long. I did it under the muse of *I am strong, and I will be strong on my own. I don't need anyone because people only hurt me* (which is a false narrative).

If we are going to fire the performer in us, odds are we will not be able to do this alone. We should not even try to go through life's journey alone. We are meant to be seen by others and to share life, even the messy, dark times. We are meant to talk and share our views and ideals. We are supposed to meander in groups, in local communities.

If you want to break up with your performer, you'll have to inform your community because relationships may depend on your performer. And as one of my favorite singers, Sam Cooke, used to say, "A change is gonna come." This change may bring integration, grieving, and may require some tough conversations.

I have a friend who was told that she was born to heal one of her mother's wounds and that the purpose of her life was to sing, dance, and be the successful one. Her family migrated to America for a better opportunity. While it sounds excellent and noble on the outside, the truth is that kind of pressure is unfair to put on a child. It's unfair to tell a child that his or her purpose is to heal me or to fulfill the dreams that I was too afraid—or unable—to go after. That child has to perform to keep the parent's approval and love, but who the hell does that child become as an adult?

If you find yourself being this child, this doesn't mean you have to break up with your parent. It means that you do, however, need to break up with the performer that they need. It's time to create and fall in love with the person you need—and that is most important.

DON'T GO WITH THE FLOW IF THAT'S NOT WHAT YOU WANT

I invite you to meet this one with a great deal of compassion because we all know how hard it can be to say no to someone, especially if you love and don't want to disappoint them and if you fear their reaction.

The latter pisses me off, and I'm so sorry for anyone who is in a situation where they have fear because of a person's reaction. I strongly suggest that you loop the community in on your fears, and again, this is hard. You may even need a new community of people to support you and hold you as you breakup with the performer.

As an empath, I often don't want to go to many places with specific people. I go because those places are safe, and I have the right to leave whenever I want. When there are group dinners, brunches, and meetings, I go because socializing is beautiful. I don't love it all the time unless it's certain people, but I still go because you never know what type of bond can come out of pushing yourself out of your shell.

Now I do have a friend I keep at a distance because this person, for lack of better description, does dumb shit often. I have too much to risk and too much on the line to be doing dumb shit. I can get a bite to eat with this person, and I love them from a distance because I just don't trust this person's judgment, but I still love them. You must be honest with yourself and make the necessary judgments so you can protect yourself, but also remember that there are some people you can love at a distance, and that's okay too.

The performer will always go with the flow even when the soul is saying it causes conflict. Fire the performer. Allow your soul to be seen.

Accept That You Do Not Need to Have It All Together

One of the most destructive practices we do is we pretend to be okay when we are not.

"Hey, how are you?"

"Fine, how are you?" In reality, he is screaming to be seen and felt. *Help me. I'm suffering. I'm upset and tired. I'm overwhelmed, and I need a safety valve. I need to get some things off my chest.*

"Okay, good, that's good. Yeah, I'm fine too."

Ha! Okay, we all have done it, right? I'm guilty as charged; however, once I fired the performer, the *fine* answer has never come out of my mouth because it's not genuine. Now, I always take moment to check-in, reflect and to give an honest answer. When you activate your soul, you stop lying, and you stop giving phony answers.

Does this mean dumping all your emotional baggage on the Whole Foods clerk as you buy your ice cream? No, Jess doesn't need to hear your whole story right now. Get your kombucha and ice cream and go home — use discernment with this practice.

Here are some phrases you can use to finesse yourself into opening up without dumping your emotional baggage on another person while respecting the essence of where you are at:

- "I'm doing the best that I can, but there are some things I should get off my chest. Do you have the capacity for that?"

- "I'd like to be 100 percent honest with you. Do you have the space for me to share how I feel?"

- And my favorite—"I am a lot of things right now. How much do you want to know because I'll tell you?"

I love all these in different ways. The key here is that we are inviting people into our wounds, thoughts, and ideas and, most importantly, inviting ourselves to be seen fully by others.

And I love the idea of not having it all together. To me, as a human, there is no such thing as complete. How can we have completeness when everything is changing? How can we be complete when it is impossible for anyone to know everything and live out every experience? We should always take on the roles of students. We are naturally curious about life, about other humans, about how processes work. The soul activates when the human experience is expanding it, so allow it to.

Your performer wants you to *act* like you have it all together, like you have all the answers. You don't. Fire your performer. Be free—be you.

Four Questions to Ask around Authenticity

I might have fear to be myself in this moment, but what if I still push myself forward? If I jumped over that fear, what would actually happen? What would happen if I kept going while fully accepting that I am afraid. Does being afraid mean I need to stop in this situation or does it mean I need to move forward?

If I keep this to myself, how will I feel? This could be magical. It could benefit others as well, so do I really want to keep it to myself, or is it more important that I take the risk of sharing?

Am I lying to myself just to be accepted by these people or by this person? Do I want to live a life where I constantly lie to myself just so I can be accepted? What will it feel like to have my truth accepted? What do I need to do in this moment to lean in closer to putting my truth out there?

How does it feel when I allow myself to not chase perfection? Can I still hold myself to a high standard without the stress of feeling like nothing will ever be enough? Am I able to push and challenge who I am but not because I think I am broken or defective? Can I challenge myself from a more loving place? Is that possible? Is it possible to give up the chase of perfection, and is it okay to be tender with myself?

You deserve to live your most authentic life. Get back in the game of life and start running the score up on them; because we win when we are authentic with ourselves. Your passions, purpose, and energy in life all go to the next level when you reclaim your authenticity. Say aloud, "This is who I am and I love me." This doesn't make you heartless, selfish, or even inconsiderate of others — no. This makes you genuine, and you are allowed to live your most authentic life — you deserve that.

—Sylvester McNutt III

When you are caught up in the future—what you should be doing and what you could do—all you do is ripen the seeds of worry and anxiety. Allow yourself to play more in the present. Embrace the unknown and curiosity.

—Sylvester McNutt III

Give yourself permission to have fun, learn, dance, sing, stretch, and use your imagination. There is no reason to be serious and stressed. Why? Who is selling us the dream that we need to chase stress? That is a sale that I need a refund for because it didn't work for me. Are you going to keep the dream of stress and worry, or are you going to give it back?

—Sylvester McNutt III

Asking for help does not make you weak—it makes you authentic. You give yourself freedom and access to higher power and information by asking questions. You dilute fear and empower courage by asking questions, by asking for help.

—Sylvester McNutt III

Throw away the idea that being strong means doing everything on your own. Real strength is building potent communities that support many people. You empower your friends, family, and community when you allow people to help you. Stop doing everything alone; instead, build a tribe and allow your journey to be witnessed by your community. Asking for help does not make you weak—it makes you authentic, it makes you a connector of people.

—Sylvester McNutt III

I'd rather be my authentic self and lose people than be a fake version of me to obtain their approval and acceptance. The right people want you to be your most authentic self. Those who don't matter want you to fake who you are just so they can say, "I like you."

—Sylvester McNutt III

Dear self,

Hope and prepare for the best. Be ready for things to go sideways as well, but stay grounded in that fact that you will remain your authentic self throughout all changes. Focus on your daily purpose and take life one day at a time.

—Sylvester McNutt III

Dear self,

Breath.

Exhale.

Relax.

I dare you to take off the mask.
I challenge you to allow your soul to show up fully, to walk into every space as your most genuine self without the need to perform or to get people to like you. I dare you to take off your mask and let people see who you truly are.

—Sylvester McNutt III

You heal the most when you are real with where you are and what you need — that is when the universe will pour into your passions, your wounds, your relationships. Self-honesty is always the key to personal freedom and liberation from the stories of our lives. Pretending to be what you are not is not authentic to your energy, and that misalignment will bring you more of what you don't want. I challenge you to throw away all the fake energy that lives inside you and show these people who you are.

—Sylvester McNutt III

Some people will like you; some won't. Do not live your life trying to get people to like you because it causes you to **present yourself**, and **you are not a presenter**. You are human, and that process has to be natural. Throw away the idea that people need to like you and let it play out as it must. Be okay with them loving you and hating you. Either outcome is not in your control — let go, and be free!

—Sylvester McNutt III

Throw away the idea that people need to like you for you to like yourself. We are off that energy.

Be you — always.

—Sylvester McNutt III • Loving Yourself Properly

Everything in your life starts with you.

If you want people to like or love the real you, then you have to commit to being your most authentic self. Be tactful and respect other people's boundaries, but don't diminish yourself just to keep others happy. We are off that—this life is beautiful and abundant, but you have to be the one to vibrate at that frequency so your life can match. Everything starts with you, so take charge and create the life you deserve.

—Sylvester McNutt III

Everything in life starts with your belief system.

The number one belief system to break away from is that *I have to be perfect* or *I must live my life to appease my parents.* You're allowed to live your life, find out who you are, and make mistakes along the way.

—Sylvester McNutt III

In the name of

self-love,

healing, and finding your
voice, all I want you to
do today is offer yourself
loving kindness and
self- compassion.
Compassion is the vessel
to heal deeply, and
you deserve that.

—Sylvester McNutt III

Can I still hold myself to a high standard without the stress of feeling like nothing will ever be enough? Am I able to push and challenge who I am but not because I think I am broken or defective? Can I challenge myself from a more loving place? Is that possible? Is it possible to give up the chase of perfection, and is it okay to be tender with myself? Is it possible that I can pursue the things I want in life without using shame, guilt or name-calling along the way?

—Sylvester McNutt III

You don't need acceptance from outsiders.

Your mission is to live your most authentic life, to figure out how to love yourself daily, and to create a safe space for others to be themselves around you. The RIGHT community will come with you on this journey as long as you stay true to yourself. Let go of the need to perform and be liked, for it doesn't serve you.

You are already free — be you.

—Sylvester McNutt III

The consequence of choosing self-love is that you choose habits, beliefs, and people who support your growth. Self-love invites you to throw away perfection, and it allows you grace. Please, give yourself the grace and patience you deserve. You are already free.

—Sylvester McNutt III

The Consequence Of Choosing Self-Love

The consequence of choosing self-love is that you choose habits, beliefs, and people who support your humanity. Self-love invites you to throw away perfection, and it allows you grace. Self-love lives in a vibrational energy field that brings clarity, healing, and self-respect. It walks shame, name-calling, and self-defeating thoughts out of your life. The consequence of choosing self-love is that how you talk to yourself will change and what you allow will, as well. Please, give yourself the grace and patience you deserve. You are already free; you are love.

- Sylvester McNutt III

The consequence of choosing self-love

with how you view yourself is that you can untangle pain from your past, you release the obsessive need to control the future, and you learn to live in this present state of mind with honor. Self-love brings you magnetic energy that heals the deepest layers of your threads. You are free — you are love. If you are ever wondering what to choose next, choose the belief and action that feels like self-love.

Sylvester McNutt III

Speak positive words into your life every single morning. Think big. Think success. Think peace. Think happiness. Think growth mindset. Always start the day with positive energy — you deserve it.

—Sylvester McNutt III

You must be willing to put yourself in a position that you deserve. Asking for clarity, direction, & opportunity is something that we all must do at some point. It's hard, and you may not get it right, but you must ask for and align yourself with everything you crave in life.

—Sylvester McNutt III

Close your eyes for a few minutes each day and imagine yourself as your highest self. Whatever that person needs to accomplish the image, give it to him or her. And whatever needs to be release, let it go peacefully. Always see yourself as your highest self — you deserve it.

—Sylvester McNutt III

In order to live your most authentic life you must preserve. You cannot quit, give up, or lose faith in yourself. You have to align with what you want, you must get your habits on the same page with your beliefs, and you must never allow failure to slow you down. Get up every single day and commit to being your real self, no matter what, push to be your highest self and trust that everything will play out.

—Sylvester McNutt III

You're not built like them, so stop trying to fit in with them. You were not put here to fit in; you are a stand out.

—Sylvester McNutt III

Living your most authentic life means that you might piss some people off. So what are you going to do? Be mad at yourself for lying and faking life, or allow them to be mad at you for whatever their reason is? Choose wisely.

—Sylvester McNutt III

6

Authentically Processing Your Emotions

NEVER FORGET THIS: AN EMOTION IS A CONSEQUENCE OF A LIVED EXPERIENCE.

Thinking about old emotions, is the analysis of a present moment that has vanished — it's gone. You are not obligated to still feel the same way now you felt when you first went through the lived experience. You are allowed to let that emotion stay in the past where it is. You are allowed to objectively observe what you have experienced (not saying you have to; just know it's available to you).

Self-love requires that we develop a safe container for our experience(s). One of the best tools for that is to ensure that we learn how to process our emotions. In this chapter, we learn how. Oftentimes we tell people to let go when we should be saying, *"I see what you are going through, and I hope you authentically process your emotions."*

Did anyone ever tell you not to cry, not to be so sensitive, not to share as much as you do? I call those people *extinguishers.* These people may mean well in some situations, and some of them may simply be mean, heartless, and unaware. Regardless of their intent, they discourage us from our full expression. They encourage us to suppress and to extinguish who we are, how we feel and what we think, our passions, our curiosities. We, too, may have been extinguishers to others without knowing it.

If you're reading this and feeling some remorse or guilt

because you did that to someone, I honor you, and I hope that you recognize that empathy is flowing through you. Only an emphatic person can recognize that they extinguished another.

No More Extinguishers

The advice to just *let it go* or *get over it* doesn't work because its bypassing the entire process of grieving, and grieving is healing. Yes, we all would love to just get over it, but telling someone — including self — to get over something that they are currently processing is not helpful. When people tell you to get over something that you are currently processing, they are actually rushing your healing process. Again they may not be doing this with ill will; however, they do need to shut the hell up respectfully (lol).

Healing cannot be rushed, it cannot be forced, it cannot be bypassed — we must allow ourselves and those around us to grieve. You cannot just get over it or let it go; you must process it. Processing can happen instantly for some, and others need to sit with it a little longer. Both are okay, but to me, the key indicator of our success is tuning in and becoming aware of **exactly what we need in that exact moment (self-love).** We have to agree that we will not allow ourselves to be extinguished moving forward, and we also have to promise to create that space for others.

Our culture doesn't make space for grieving—I mean, yes, we go to funerals; but outside of that, where are we allowed to go to grieve?

I love grieving because the process lets me know that I'm alive; it lets me know that I feel something through my bones and soul. Grieving allows me to honor what or whom I lost, and I'm so grateful that humans have this power to grieve. I'm so grateful that we have the ability to authentically process what we are going through.

My friend Janet is studying to be a doctor; she's almost done with the program. She said something that was so profound to me today as we were texting about life. "I just don't have the capacity to be emotionally supportive to anyone right now, and I feel guilty about that, but the truth is I just don't have it."

I said, "Janet, that is one of the most beautiful things I've ever heard. You're actually acknowledging where you are in life. You are allowing yourself to process your emotions authentically, and that is giving you a clear direction in your life. It sounds like this is a time when you need to focus on your healing and your boundaries. Knowing that you have a loving and giving heart, when the time comes to welcome people into your space, I'm sure you will."

"Damn, I needed that reassurance. I've been struggling with this all week, so much so that I broke down crying because of the guilt and shame. The reassurance you just gave me makes me feel lighter," she said.

In her life, she doesn't have the capacity for much emotional support, and I see nothing wrong with being honest with where you are. The problem is that many of us fail to directly pinpoint where we are, how we feel, and what our capacity is—we extinguish our own voice and our own body oftentimes because we were taught to do that by parents who did it.

I think it comes down to many of us putting a suppressor on our emotions; it comes down to the fact that we aren't allowed to process the full gamut of human emotions in public either. We cheer on happiness, love, and joy. We shame anger, pain, sadness, and confusion. Our work here is to become aware of all emotions and to give ourselves permission to be honest with who we are and where we are.

Two Things Happen When You Authentically Process Your Emotions

First, they pass, as they should, without forcing any emotion to stay. This is also how we can make sure that our ego and identity never get wrapped up in fleeting emotions. Once we practice acknowledging them, then we allow them to disperse because we recognize the impermanence of each moment (feeling, accepting, and letting go).

Secondly, feeling them gives me honest feedback on my life, which ends overthinking, anxiety, and unneeded fear. Practicing self-honesty brings you a great deal of humanity and grace as well. If you lie to yourself and others about what you feel, what your boundaries are, and what you're going through, your body knows.

Your body holds on to that lie and forms energy around it. Your body creates tightness and stress because it isn't allowed the grace to be human, to heal, to grow. This is why being honest with yourself is a step toward freedom—you deserve that.

Healing cannot be rushed; it cannot be forced; it cannot be bypassed or skipped because we assume the next level feels better. *You cannot just get over it* or l*et it go;* you must process it, grieve it, and make an authentic space for that thing to fade naturally. You're allowed to grieve at a pace that feels most comfortable to you. True healing does not have a timetable — it flows based on you, where you are in life, and the depth of the bonds of the situation at hand. Do not minimize your pain either because someone you know got over it faster or better than you; no, never do that. Your healing is not up for competition with anyone. You are free from competing, forcing, and rushing yourself. Your healing is a sacred practice, and as long as you fully acknowledge what you need and want, you are doing it right. Be compassionate and kind to yourself on this journey — you deserve that.

Why Process?

One word: *completion.*

In our society, people chase goals because they think it's going to lead them to this emotional state of completion, and these goals help, but the circle is never complete. Why? It's because we've spent years ignoring our own body, our own mind. We have so much residue left that our machines aren't operating as optimally as they should.

And then combine that with poor dietary choices, sedentary lifestyles, negligence of sleep, substance abuse, and addiction to added sugar and other foods that lower our vibration, and what do you have? You have an adult who has never processed his or her own life and whose body is not in total alignment with health, vitality, and healing. You have an adult who doesn't even know that they need healing, but they do —they need it deeply.

Let me be clear when I say "completion." I believe that healing is the key to success, and when I say "success," I also like to intertwine that word with purpose or direction. This is one of my deepest and strongest convictions in life: healing is the key to success. Often in our society, success is about reaching an end point or desired outcome, and I tend to see it as that as well. However, I also see success as a direction, as a journey, as a path. Success to me is an *and*, not an *or*. It can be both *the journey* and *the destination.*

Our culture is obsessed with money, so much so that we worship the dollar, physical garments, and things that will bring us a perceived status. We know millionaires who aren't substantially happy, even though they have all the money in the world. Why? We know people who are in a great relationship in social media, but in real life, they know that their relationship is just an aesthetic, performative vessel to try to fill some void. We know someone who has something that others look at and marvel, and secretly, they are dealing with all the things we have talked about so far (shame, unprocessed emotions, etc.). And let me be clear—I am not shaming people who are wealthy or who share their relationships online; however, I just feel like those archetypes are sought after by many without recognizing the full complexity of the experience, that's all.

So the question is, how do we bring healing to our relationship? How do we bring fulfillment to that millionaire whose emptiness has been multiplied by his or her net worth. How do we—as we sit in coffee shops, at the beach, or at dinner with our family—begin to bring the depth of healing that we deserve to our lives? My answer: *completion.*

SPIRITUAL BYPASSING

Spiritual bypassing is a term that was coined by a well-known psychologist named John Welwood. It is the act of using spiritual beliefs or phrases to avoid facing our painful feelings and unmet needs. It is a very persistent shadow of spirituality, which initiates us into a state of avoidance, resistance, and repression. An article in *Psychology Today* written by Diane Raab, PhD, defines *spiritual bypassing* as using spiritual ideas and practices to sidestep emotional "unfinished business". Spiritual bypassing is said to be used to stir up a shaky sense of self by belittling basic needs, unhealed trauma, and developmental tasks.

When we practice presence and when we dive into whatever comes up, it becomes easier to deal with the goings-on of the human experience. The avoidance, repression, and hiding of the elephant in the room, as they say, is what makes life hard—and this moment is an invitation to stop doing that. In fact, we talked about extinguishing earlier. It's safe to say that extinguishing the behavior of spiritual bypassing is one that we are okay with. Our work here is to make a commitment to not run from the work that we have to do, and our work is about allowing ourselves to be present because when we are present, we cannot run, nor do we want to.

Why is it important?

Spiritual bypassing is dangerous because it sets up a split within a person. Most people believe that spirituality is supposed to be an adventure of integration, but if you bypass the truthfulness of your pain, you will only arrive at the happiness of your lies. Eventually your false sense of self will fold in on itself, and so will the false sense of happiness it was attached to—disintegration. When left unchecked, it creates a division between where you are and where you think you should be.

To avoid this fall into the darkness, we urge people to meet themselves in their most honest form. There are many traditions people use to accomplish this form of honesty. Unfortunately, many of these traditions—such as religious groups—sometimes justify living in a state of inauthenticity or "impurity," and therefore it is something we all need to understand if we are to reverse the repression and authentically grow into accurate projections of ourselves. If we do not outgrow bypassing, then the depth of any spiritual teaching will not be truly expressed. It is important to know what spiritual bypassing is because it is one of the biggest problems in mainstream spirituality today, causing many people to feel like impostors in their spiritual awakening while also avoiding and delaying the healing they actually need—and are deserving of.

Too often in my community, I've heard leaders and teachers tell people, "Oh well, just move on." After reading this full chapter, you now know how to process and why it's so important, I'm sure. Bypassing is equivalent to dismissive positivity. The truth is telling people to move on needs to be accompanied with context and the right type of storytelling, skills, and the right containment for them. It must also create a compassionate space so people can move on gently. Moving on is a process of being real with ourselves above all else, of living our most authentic life.

What if I use Affirmations, is that Spiritual Bypassing?

This solely depends on one thing: are you acknowledging what has or is happening? I love affirmations and I believe that they are strongly necessary to transform, to grow and to process life. In fact, I've used them all throughout this book.

Words have the power to signal your DNA to grow, to evolve, to create your destiny. Through the power of words your body can feel a lived experience without actually living it. You can feel the consequences of a lived experience by using words — that's how powerful they are. So, yes, I love affirmations and I also love when we choose to acknowledge *what is* because that acknowledgment of what is gives us the ability to see the totality of the experience.

Release Your Limiting Emotions

What would happen if we choose to release the limiting emotions that we have made secret contracts with? I wonder how that would impact us and our relationships?

Dr. Joe Dispenza says, "When you look at those emotions and you begin to un-memorize those emotions, then you begin to liberate energy. Every time you liberate an emotion you're closing the gap between how you appear to the world and how you are inside of you. Every time you un-memorize an emotion, you liberate energy. And that is available energy for you to create a new destiny with."

Think about it like this. Everything is energy. The places you go, the people you choose to be around, the habits you have, the things you buy, the places you eat all have an energetic connection with you.

You go to the same restaurant because you have an energetic bond there. You've had experiences there, and you like the consequences of those experiences, which is the emotion you felt while there or once you returned home. The outcome of our lived experiences are our emotions, and our feelings create attachments and bonds. So that is why you go over and over — you're choosing the energy bond.

If you want to command your new future, one laced with self-love and authenticity, you have to visit those emotional bonds that are bound through misery, pain, self-defeating thoughts, and limiting emotions. As you begin to un-memorize these emotions, you create new energy that you can use to create the life you want. As a consequence of reconditioning the feelings you experience, you will break the bonds, allowing you to choose new experiences. Once you overcome emotions, you snap the bond from the past, and once you snap the bond, you now have new energy to use.

I told you a few pages ago that I grew up with alcoholic parents and some other things that aren't worth mentioning again. But, when I repeated this story over and over (when I was deep in those wounds and much younger), every single person in my life, too, had those deep wounds, and they too dealt with the shame, fear, and all of the emotions that I lived at.

But as I healed, changed, and outgrew that story, my vibrational frequency changed. The energetic magnet inside of me shifted, and now, the people in my life do not operate in that victim mentality either. Now, I meet people with emotional intelligence, sober people, or people who exhibit appropriate alcohol behaviors. None of the people in my life believe in child abuse. The people in my life are like me: focused on healing, success, and enjoying this majestic life. My life is external proof that energy and the thoughts matter. Even when I was in my deepest depression, suffering in that house with them I knew there was a way out. I knew there was a better life. I knew that environment was not in alignment with me.

Why? Because of Energy

So what happened? What happened is I authentically processed the emotions of my trauma, and by choosing to let them go, I let go of the story that I was telling myself (which was reinforcing the feelings). If we believe that we can overcome our emotions, then and only then will we begin to live our most authentic life. My life now is a pure reflection of the energetic thoughts that I believed in, even when I was going through the deepest heartbreak—the heartbreak of recognizing that your parents do not have the capacity to protect you.

One level deeper: I am not an alcoholic, thankfully and I have a deep compassion for anyone who is. I don't drink alcohol (200 days sober at the time of this writing). I consider myself a sober curious person because I am not sure what my relationship will be with alcohol in the future, but I don't drink today. I'd like to reach this first year of sobriety and then undertake a period of deep internal reflection to see what my body and soul is asking fo me. I'll update you about this journey on my podcast, and of course, in the next book!

I have a vibrant and loving son, and I don't believe in spankings as a form of discipline. Why? Because I experienced it, and it made no sense to me, especially because spankings under the influence of alcohol go to a level that no child should experience. A parent's key role is to create a safe environment for the offspring and to be conscious of what habits and belief systems we are passing. I believe in passing curiosity, speaking up on your wants and needs, wanderlust adventures, life-long learning, and participating in an integrated community. There are other ways to show a human consequence without violence, and that is why I do not believe in violence as a form of leadership, personally.

And lastly, I do consider myself financially free, not because of how much money I have but because of how I live my life (not addicted to consumerism, low expenses, and high income). I am most proud of these three states of mind because I had to fight the story, self-defeating thoughts, environment, and had to elect the choice of a higher vibration to create this state of mind.

My son, Mason, is now growing up in this nurturing environment — and this is called changing your family tree and breaking generational curses. This power is inside of you, too; otherwise, you wouldn't have seen these words. You can profoundly influence your destiny simply by being aware of your thoughts and breaking the emotional bonds that trap you.

You are already free!

You are already free!

You are already free!

You are already free!

You are already free!

You are already free!

To love deeply

means that you also must love endings and not just the parts that appease your story and ego. It means that we must learn how to grieve, how to honor what and who is no longer present, and how to find a deep gratitude for the presences that have touched our souls.

—Sylvester McNutt III

Honor the ending

of your relationships. Bring your most sincere love and self-respect to the end. This is how you obtain closure and process what has occurred maturely. This is how you move on and grieve, respectfully. Do not bring toxic energy to the endings — you have too much at stake to do so.

—Sylvester McNutt III

I love grieving because the process lets me know that I'm alive; it lets me know that I feel something through my bones and soul. Grieving allows me to honor what or whom I lost, and I'm so grateful that humans have this power to grieve, to reflect, to cook the emotions of endings and change.

—Sylvester McNutt III

If you are used to running away from tough conversations, as you start practicing them more, you may need to reward yourself for attempting to enter those conversations that you used to hide from. Self-encouragement goes a long way. Affirm and say, “Self, I am proud of you for trying to meet that conversation that you would’ve run from last year.” Acknowledge your small steps!

—Sylvester McNutt III

Dear self,

you are worthy of solving all conflicts in your life. At times we can hide from tough conversations or emotions that come up, and we act like we don't need anyone and like we have it all together. Meanwhile we suffer on the inside. Affirm, "I have the power to face the darkness, to learn from it, and to come out more potent on the other side."

—Sylvester McNutt III

You Are Free From The Old Story

You will expand into your highest potential once you break up with the emotions that keep you in the past. **How**: *recognize that your biography doesn't serve you and grieve your past.* What is in direct alignment is choosing beliefs, patterns, and environments that align with your potential! If possible, forgive yourself and others from your past so you can release the emotional residue of these old stories that come into your present day. Be patient and kind with yourself as you attempt to forgive and grieve the past.

—Sylvester McNutt III

Free yourself

from the idea that ignoring your emotions is going to somehow make it okay later; it won't, and you know it. Your unacknowledged emotions turn into a volcano, and then they erupt later, and that eruption is destructive for your life. Get in the practice of staying present, breathing deeply when things arise, and learning how to authentically process what you're feeling so it can fade as it's naturally supposed to.

—Sylvester McNutt III

You have immense power inside you – so massive that you can dictate your future with your thought and intention. You have the power to change your personal reality. You have the magnetic energy to shift your behaviors and outcomes.

Claim this magnetic energy!

—Sylvester McNutt III

You don't have to entertain the *bullshit & the struggle* anymore. That energy is your old story, old body, old way of living. By seeing these words you have already given yourself new energy to use. With compassion, and no shame allow yourself to refocus and spend your time choosing self-love.

—Sylvester McNutt III

7

Create A Nurturing Inner Voice

SELF-LOVE REQUIRES THAT YOU DEVELOP AN ENCOURAGING INNER VOICE.

How you talk to yourself and about yourself can support you, or it can destroy your confidence—learning how to create a nurturing inner voice is critical to our journey. In this chapter, we talk about how to unlearn an inner voice that isn't helpful, and we learn how to create a voice that moves us toward a more loving vibration.

September 2010—Derrick Martell Rose was asked, "Hey, Derrick, you won the Rookie of the Year award. You made your first all-star team a year ago. Now people around the league talk about you taking the next jump to become a top ten player in the league. I know you've never been one to back away from a challenge. What types of expectations do you set for yourself going into year three?"

Derrick, a usually reserved and quiet twenty-one-year-old, used an affirmation to explain his expectations of himself. He said, "It's high." He looked at the podium for a few seconds, and you can tell he was gathering up the strength to speak what he feels in his heart. "The way I look at it within myself, why not? Why can't I be the MVP of the league? Why can't I be the best player in the league? I don't see why [not]. Why can't I do that? I think I work hard. I think I dedicate myself to the game and sacrifice a lot of things at a young age, and I know, if I continue to do good, what I can get out of it."

To be the most valuable player in any league requires a great deal of consistency, effort, and grit. To become the most valuable asset in an organization, a lot of situations have to go right. We've used the words several times in *Loving Yourself Properly*, but this is about making yourself a more potent adult. To be valuable, one must be willing to share their heart, to put out effort, and to show up to the task at hand with the most potent mindset and energy.

At age twenty-two, Rose was named the youngest MVP in NBA history. At the end of the season, he ran away with the voting in a landslide; Rose collected 113 of 120 first-place votes, which was almost unanimous. Basketball and statistics nerds will argue about the actual numbers. Still, I can tell you this with extreme confidence—Rose won that MVP award because of the press conference that he had at the start of the season, with the words of affirmation he put out in the universe and then the effort that backed them up. The entire narrative of that season was built by that declaration he made, and the same can be done for us.

When he made a declaration by saying, "Why can't I be MVP?" the entire world moved around him to help him conspire the reality that he claimed he wanted — all he did was express a self-affirming belief. I strongly believe in the law of attraction, which is speaking what you want into existence; however, I take it much further. The law of attraction without action is nothing but a dream, and dreams do not become reality without action, without the effort, and without showing up over and over for yourself and others.

This is one of the most potent stories around using your voice because Derrick is also quiet and reserved. He is the prime example of *mean what you say*. You do not have to be an extrovert to have a strong voice, nor do you need to have a big personality, but you need to use your voice and words wisely. Using your words in a friendly manner toward yourself will earn you an MVP award, in your life—and that is how you must look at it.

The more potent we are, the better for our team, family, and community. Most look at an MVP award and think *individual*, but we should not—we are out here for the team. Any individual award—real, imaginative, or even used as an allegory for us—is all about the team, the whole. We may view this as an individualistic achievement, but it's not if we think holistically about it. And for our journey here, regardless of environment, personality test scores, what matters most to us is that our beliefs create our lived experiences. The consequence of all lived experience is an emotion and how we choose to see the world comes from how we authentically process our emotions — do you see how this all comes together now?

***

Wearing headphones is an exciting experience, especially the over-ear headphones with good bass. When you listen to music, you are agreeing to allow someone else's vibrations to come through your skull. You tune in to their drums, high hats, and guitars, as well as the pitch and tone of their voice, if there are words. You choose to allow your soul and body to align with the story that they are telling through the words.

Think about your go-to artist when you go through depressive eras of your life. Why is that? Odds are they are singing about sad content—it aligns, so it's a choice to tune into that vibration. And that sad music makes you feel comfortable, or you just hear a vibration that aligns with your present state, and that brings healing because it helps us feel like you aren't alone.

The same applies when you watch a movie. You have no idea what the character is about to do, who they are about to meet, or what story line they are about to work themselves through. But you still watch, and in the end, you cheer for them as soon as you develop a connection with them.

When you listen to a song, you hope that it's good and that it makes you feel good. And if the words are powerful enough, you'll feel connected to the emotion of the words. In the movies, you root for all the characters you like to win, and if they do not end up with a happy ending, your feelings are affected. We all love a good story where a character goes through hell but comes out on top after figuring out how to mitigate problems. So my question is, why do we want our favorite musician to craft a song that is timeless and perfect? Why do we want characters in movies to overcome their struggle? Why do we allow them in our heads, root for them, and become their cheerleader, *but then we refuse to give that same energy to ourselves?*

Huh, oh yeah, gut punch isn't it. I want to know why. I want you to stop and question yourself, "Why is that? Why do we go out of our way to want the best for other people genuinely, and when the lens is on us, we don't want to be seen in that light? Why?"

This is one of the most profound questions that we will ever ask ourselves. Do we not deserve to be our cheerleaders? Do we not deserve to root for ourselves? Do we not deserve that same timeless bliss that a musician feels when making a song that will last across the ages? Are we unworthy of love and encouragement? Should we only aim to please and give love away and to never take it back? Is it honestly what we came to this life to do?

You will never forget the pages that you just read, and because of that, you now must create a nourishing inner voice. This is your duty. This is the biggest responsibility you will undertake as you exit this mindset. You must agree to use a nurturing inner voice and to let go of the non-nurturing inner voice that may be roaming around you. At this very moment, I want you to say aloud," "I release the non-nurturing inner voice, and I no longer give it permission to be inside me. I am free. I am releasing everything that is less than love."

For whatever reason, we have fallen in love with the idea of perfectionism and the high expectations that come with it. As of this moment, we are curious students choosing to break up with that idea because it doesn't serve us in the life that we want to live anymore.

Over the final pages of this chapter, you will see heart-crafted affirmations that will empower you to nurture your inner voice. I challenge you to say these aloud so your entire body can register the words which will program your destiny. But before anything else, I want to break down *how* we can understand this practice.

You Repeat Negative Thoughts, but You Don't Have to (Conditioning)

Before I explain, say aloud, "I am free from repeating negative thoughts, that belongs to my old way of thinking and my old body. This present version of me uses self-affirming-loving language."

You have most likely been lying to yourself through conditioning, especially when it comes to the thoughts you allow yourself to attach to your energy field. Often our thoughts in the present come from past moments, feelings, or stories. Those attachments to the past keep popping up in our present, but they don't have to.

We have the power today to break free, to deliver our energy from them. There is a term in psychology called *classical conditioning*, and it represents how we learn what consequences will happen after particular actions and behaviors, learning through association. Two stimuli are linked together to produce a new learned response in a person or animal in simple terms. If you see a therapist, talk to a life coach, or deal with anyone who works in transformation, one way or another, they are using these principles to help you see a new truth, a new image of your life, by using the prime matter (the material that is already present in your life and that can be cooked, worked, or used to create a shift).

If you take away all the labels and stories in life and if you objectively observe what is happening, you'll see that life is nothing more than stimulus and response. It's simple yet profound to us because for many of us, seeing life in such a simple way, is not realistic. But that is what it is.

We have been conditioned to give ourselves these multilayered identities (ego), but are those identities real? How long does an identity hold for us? I don't know. I am asking. My identity may and will change (I hope), but no matter who I become, I will still be a human being who lives off stimulus and response—simplicity at its finest. This is why living in the present is agreed upon by all spiritual teachers and one of the most potent practices. Also, this is why the power of words is so important because the words we choose manifest our destiny, so should we choose *self-defeating* thoughts of *self-nurturing?*

People who have insecurities, who lack confidence, and who do not practice self-love are continually telling themselves how or why they are not good enough, which is also a practice of grading that comes from observing the past with the wrong view or projecting what we should be in the future. But today we can and we will choose to break up with that by choosing to fire the unhelpful coach that lives inside us and hiring a new one. Does this happen instantly? Maybe for you it might. Will it take practice? Yes, that is possible too. Please give yourself compassion as you work on shifting your inner voice. You are a being of love, and that is what you deserve to hear most often.

Fire Your Unhelpful Coach

Your critical inner voice can get in your way if you do not treat it as you will another person. It is important to set healthy boundaries and develop that voice to be an ally only and never an enemy. Tamsen Firestone, the author of *Daring to Love*, says that the critical inner voice is a by-product of the defenses we developed as children to cope with any stressful or painful events. The voice was born early on when we were vulnerable youngsters trying to protect ourselves against frustration and emotional pain, reinforced throughout childhood and adolescence, and even in our adulthood.

As a new father, I can tell you that my son needs me to protect himself and keep himself alive. When we play, he grabs me for leverage to sit and stand up properly; he looks into my eyes to confirm his behavior (stimulus and response). He doesn't know if his behavior is bad or good based on the world I live in, but he does look at me to see how I react to him. For him, everything is an experiment, and he's testing everything to help him figure out how to function in his body and this world. My daily choices grow his inner voice, his perception of self, and his confidence. Like we talked about earlier, our relationship genuinely comes down to stimuli and responses. As a parent, one of our most extraordinary responsibilities is to develop an awareness of how we may or may not be influencing our children.

But what about that little boy that we talked about earlier, the one who suffered in Chicago, the little boy who didn't have a healthy home environment? How do we think his inner voice was? What can that little boy, who is now an adult, do to change his relationship with the inner voice? No matter what we went through in our youth, we still have a duty now as conscious people to choose our inner voice—again this may not be easy, but difficulty is not our target; we are here to focus on what is necessary. Some of us may need to do a great reconstruction of our voice, and if that is where you are, then get ready for the undertaking.

If you look around our present day, it's evident that most adults are still walking around in their adolescent mindset and voice. In Francis Weller's lecture *The Alchemy of Initiation*, he talks about how there is no demarcation point in our society where adults are born. There's no actual process or ritual that we go through that gives us a graduation ceremony into adulthood.

The theory that we are not adults because we still have childlike consciousness makes 100 percent sense to me.

What about you? Do you know any children who show up in adult bodies? I bet you do. If we operate with immature patterns, like an undeveloped inner voice, it makes sense why anxiety and depression are present-day issues, and I say that compassionately. It makes sense why relationships suffer, why our family structures have generational toxicity that gets passed on, and why we are so out of shape as a society—we don't feel worthy of anything better, and we have not been challenged to increase our potency.

The critical inner voice—another nemesis that aims to stop us from developing our potency and self-love, the voice that prevents us from showing up fully in our community—must be defeated. I am challenging you to destroy the nemesis of a toxic inner voice and to allow a new one to be born. Do you accept?

How to Break Up with Repeating Negative Thoughts:

Allow yourself to recognize the thought patterns.

You must ask yourself where the energy behind these thoughts came from. Is this your thought? Does this come from a past lesson? Has a parent, society, or someone who is not even in your life given you this idea about yourself? It's crucial to your journey to determine if this is an original thought or someone else's that you have just repeated. Knowing the source helps you abolish it much quicker.

We have talked about stimulus and response earlier; bring that into your journey as you examine yourself. In your very first step, you do not have to fix or change anything. The first step is only about recognition, allowing yourself to tap into the highest self-awareness level without judgment and grading.

Ask yourself, "Do I have to hold this thought?"

Am I allowed to be free from this thought? Am I allowed to move on from this thought? Am I allowed to start repeating different thoughts to myself, thoughts that are more positive and encouraging?

In my heart, I would love to tell you that you do not have to hold any thoughts as truth, but you must arrive at this conclusion on your own, on your time. Do you have to hold on to thoughts that do not help you? This part is about permitting yourself to allow your thoughts to flow and pass as they naturally do.

Practice saying positive thoughts aloud

Self-criticism is the enemy, and to beat the enemy, you need to bring the biggest missile possible to the fight. In this war, the best bomb you can drop is your voice. Self-criticism cannot win against a confident voice; it can't. It's proven that speaking to yourself aloud can make your statements more powerful.

Gary Lupyan from the University of Wisconsin–Madison calls the phenomenon "feedback hypothesis." Along with his team, the researcher conducted an experiment that asked subjects to go through a stack of photographs and look for a photo of a particular, assigned object. According to the *New York Times*, if they said the name of whatever object out loud while looking, they tended to find the image faster. This is why saying phrases, affirmations, and ideas to yourself aloud can significantly benefit your fight against self-criticism. Practice saying the things that uplift and motivate you to be your highest self.

Jack Canfield says daily affirmations are simple positive statements declaring specific goals in their completed states. These empowering mantras have profound effects on the conscious and unconscious mind. Daily affirmations are what exercise is to the body; I recommend doing them every morning and every night before bed. I do them twice a day and have done that for over a decade. To me, it is one of the best practices that I do daily.

Use A Loving Voice

Please, just let love into your life by always choosing a loving voice that builds and never destroys. Start with your voice: how you decide to talk about yourself, your life, and how the world is everything. There is no reason to talk about yourself or beat yourself. Language is one of the most powerful tools we have; use it to intensify your exquisite life. Use affirmations to affirm and support your health and vitality. Use positive words to encourage you to continue your pursuit of truth and authenticity. Use laughter to disarm yourself and others and to make situations lighter. Use your tone of voice to connect and to establish trust. When speaking about yourself, always choose love.

—Sylvester McNutt III

"I Am My Own Worst Critic"

No, you are not — stop saying this. Your natural voice is a loving and curious one; that is who you were as a child. Your society or your family system is what taught you that it wasn't okay to make mistakes, to be a growing human who doesn't always make the "best" choice. Self-love for you at this moment is recognizing that you must break up with the mindset of I am my own worst critic because that isn't your voice you hear when you are critiquing yourself. It's a parent or a society that didn't use empathy and love. Use this moment to come back to your body, to breathe, to forgive yourself for using that voice. Going forward, you will practice using a loving and empathic voice towards yourself. You are not a critic; you are a supporter.

—Sylvester McNutt III

Stop Being Critical Of Your Art and Yourself

You are art. Art is here to be a vessel for us to play in, express, and connect to a deeper version of our existence. The composition of the photo does not need to be perfect. The dance does not have to be robotic. The yoga pose is not about how flexible you are. The poem that you're scared to share may save a life when you utter the words. Every day we get to see art in the form of ocean waves, babies smiling, and sunsets that splash across the horizon. We are not here to be perfect, correct, or compete – we are here to express ourselves authentically. The most authentic you is more than enough. We are here to learn and to love life deeply.

—Sylvester McNutt III

You Are One Genuine Apology Away From Freedom

If you sit back and realize that the inner voice you use today is not a loving one, odds are, it came from your family system or society. Today, I want you to forgive your family system and yourself. Offer your parents the most sincere apology possible — even if you feel like they are undeserving. This apology isn't about them; ***it's about you and your healing process.*** The apology is the first step towards letting go of the voice you've developed an attachment to. The apology is a step towards empathy, and the number one vessel for us to use on our self-love journey is empathy. Our responsibility as healing, growing, and sovereign beings are to abolish mindsets and practices that do not call us into our highest vibration. You are free from the critical inner voices. You will use love, empathy, and kindness towards yourself — you deserve this. Release everything that is less than love.

—Sylvester McNutt III

8

Self-Love Affirmations

Affirm:

I am here to play life big, think enormous possibilities about what I can do, and take big risks as I learn about life. I am here to make mistakes, put myself out there, and persevere no matter how hard something is. I am here to make a difference and to always go for the life that I deserve. This is the season for going for everything that I want — no matter what. The universe is here to work for me and with me. Opportunity will find me daily, because my frequency is the highest it can be.

—Sylvester McNutt III

Affirm:

I do not need validation for what I want to achieve in life. I do not expect people to understand *why* I need to do what I need to do. However, I do expect myself to go for everything that I want. I'm built differently than most people, and that is okay. That doesn't make me *better* or *worse*; I don't think like that — I accept that each person has something unique about them, and I choose to honor my uniqueness. But I know that I am different because of how my heart and passionate demeanor are set up. I know that my passion fuels me and gives me the energy to manifest the life I want. I am so grateful for those who take time to hear me, to get to know me, who make sacred space for me to share with them. I also know that some do not have the capabilities, and that is okay. I am at peace through all things in my life.

—Sylvester McNutt III

Affirm:

My life can be whatever I choose it be. I have thoughts that matter, a voice that people want to hear, and a presence that makes others feel welcome. I am a person who wants to learn and grow. I am choosing to be the most potent version of myself. I love who I am, today.

—Sylvester McNutt III

Affirm:

Self-love flows through my energy field daily. I am worthy of going after the life I deserve. I will not play small because my soul, heart, and passion for life are simply too damn big for that.

—Sylvester McNutt III

Affirm:

I am worthy of enjoying my hard work, success, and happiness, and I do not have to feel bad when I have it. I have fought for the life that I have and I deserve to enjoy it. I am blessed and grateful for this journey. I sit here before you with gratitude and love for what my life is.

—Sylvester McNutt III

Affirm: I will take time to remember and honor my accomplishments. I will acknowledge the people who have helped me along my path because we are not alone. I will push forward and go for the life I deserve as a way to honor those who have invested in me.

Affirm: I am so happy and grateful that I am living the life that I have worked for. I am allowed to savor this life with people I love as well. I'm proud of myself that I never gave up, and damn, I am so appreciative of those who always believed in me — thank you.

—Sylvester McNutt III

Affirm:

I believe that I will achieve everything that I am imagining. I believe things will work out for me, even when there is turbulence or resistance. I believe that I will think big when it comes to success. Most people think too small, and I deserve to keep my thoughts big. I am worthy of going after my big dreams no matter how hard it may be.

—Sylvester McNutt III

Affirm:

I am in control of my destiny. I take action to create the life I want, for action is better than reaction or no action. I let go of what I cannot control, and I keep my focus on what I can impact: my belief system, my actions, and how I show up in life.

—Sylvester McNutt III

Affirm:

I'm so happy and thankful that I keep my mind in a heightened state of focus, clarity, and determination. I give my best to the world because serving people is important to me. The only thing I want to give to this life is my best version of me. I have a lot to offer and I get such a great feeling out of serving, helping and giving. Giving to the community is everything for me.

—Sylvester McNutt III

Affirm:

I am so happy that I have the power to choose who I want to be. I do not have to be what society wants, what my family wants, or what people who don't care about me want. I have the ability to choose to be who I want. I am beyond grateful for this mindset. I forgive all past versions of myself and I must honor them by being my most authentic self today. My soul is free.
—Sylvester McNutt III

Affirm:

I attract everything that I require. The power to get everything I want is already inside of me. I am a magnet for success, happiness, and joy. I am in alignment with nature, the earth, and the soil. I am not here to chase material things and status. I'm here to root deep into my purpose, serve, and be a vessel of love for those who co-create space with me.

—Sylvester McNutt III

Affirm:

I am passionately driven by family, community, relationships, and connection. I have to keep going for everything I want in life because it's bigger than me. I want the best for me, my community, and my family tree. I was chosen to change my family tree, take risks, and push for the highest energy level possible. My story isn't about me solely; it's about the community and those who hold me close to their heart. I have to show up for them, for their honor and legacy. I want this for me too, of course, but nothing is more important than community to me.

— Sylvester McNutt III

Affirm:

I use gratitude everyday because it is a multiplier, and I recognize that there is a lot for me to be grateful for. I have a wonderful life and I am a magnetic for love, connection and community. I'm so appreciative for what my life is and where I am at in this moment.

—Sylvester McNutt III

Affirm:

I'm so happy and grateful that I continue to heal deeply from the pain that used to torment me. I am proud of what I have overcome, and I love who I am today. I am grateful that I am no longer trapped in that story — I am free, and happy.

—Sylvester McNutt III

Affirm:

I'm so fortunate and grateful

that I continue my healing process at a pace that feels safe for me. I am loving the person I am becoming. I am so proud of what I have shed and what I have let go of. I'm allowing myself to stay present and grateful for my soul, my body, and my emotions in this moment.

—Sylvester McNutt III

Affirm:

I am so happy and grateful that I allow myself to heal when I need it. I listen to my body, I trust my intuition, and I give myself what I need to heal and to stay vibrant.

—Sylvester McNutt III

Affirm:

I am so happy and grateful

for all the energy that flows through me. I am proud to know that I have vitality and strength. I don't get tired of life because I am inspired, driven, focused, and ready to live fully. I'm so happy and appreciative that I am feeling a deep inner peace. I love the calmness that flows through my life. I'm accepting my past for what it is and I'm choosing to honor myself, my ancestors, and my community by giving myself as much grace as possible.

—Sylvester McNutt III

Affirm:

By loving myself I attract what I desire; I create a magical world based on the most powerful emotion and energy. I am a magnet for love from others and I have more than enough love to give. People treat me well and I try my best to return the good energy to them. The consequence of self-love is a life that consistently adjusts and returns to balance — I deserve that.

— Sylvester McNutt III

Affirm:

I observe my energy choices closely

I am mindful of where I put my attention and energy. Focusing on negative and low vibrational thoughts creates a life that follows that energy. I choose love, healing, and the life of beauty, so I am mindful of where I put my attention to make sure that I am in alignment. I observe where I put my energy choices closely — this matters to me, in all pillars of my life.

—Sylvester McNutt III

Affirm:

I envision big and bold outcomes

I am mindful of how I envision my outcomes. I focus on doing well, moving forward, and succeeding. I see myself and my community thriving and loving deeply. I see us moving past adversity, working together and respecting each person's power. I envision that conflict will get dealt with safely and properly. I envision us all winning, and winning big.

—Sylvester McNutt III

Affirm:

I'm mindful of how I spend my days

I am mindful of how I spend my days, and each day I will stop and find time to be grateful. I will find time to be thankful for little things like access to clean water, breathable air, and a body that works. I am grateful and happy about how I choose to spend my time. I cherish each day, and I do not take anything for granted. I live each day humbly for what I have while I honor and love what and whom I have lost.

—Sylvester McNutt III

Affirm:

I'm so grateful for who I get to spend time with

I am mindful of who I spend time with. I want to share safe spaces with people where we can both grow and thrive. I will align with the people who also operate at this frequency. I will enter and participate in high functioning and safe for everyone environments. I love being around people who uplift, inspire and make me laugh and I hope to provide that safe space for many.

—Sylvester McNutt III

Affirm:

Touch Is Everything

I am mindful of who I allow to touch me. Touch is an intimate exchange of senses, energy, and connection. I am selective about who has access to my skin. I am empathic to other's energy and my own, because of this I have to be specific with who is allowed to touch me. Touch is love; touch is a wonderful language. I love touching when I trust the person's energy.

—Sylvester McNutt III

Affirm:

I am free from overthinking

I will allow myself to be free from overthinking. I will take a few seconds to breathe and laugh, and I will allow thoughts to pass. At this moment, I am choosing peace of mind over stress. I am no longer focused on controlling outcomes, people or narratives. What is for me will always find me, and therefore, there is no reason to overthink. I am free from overanalyzing and guessing what will play out — I am totally free, living in a deep acceptance of what is and what is not.

-- Sylvester McNutt III

Affirm:

I am free from overthinking

I am grateful to know that I am free from overthinking. I will allow answers to flow through me. I will allow ideas and thoughts to work together to guide me on the most appropriate path. I will sit with discomfort and uneasiness to enable the answers to come to me. And I respect and acknowledge that sometimes, there will be no answers — and that is okay too.

—Sylvester McNutt III

Affirm:

I am proud of my journey

I'm proud because my healing process is going just as it should. I honor when I am not well, and I lean into the days that feel like abundance. There's a rhythm and flow to it in my life. I am grateful that my life keeps giving me reasons to dance, to play, to wander. I respect my mind and honor that my process will play out as it should.

—Sylvester McNutt III

Affirm:

Emotionally, I am free

I am comfortable sharing my feelings, thoughts and ideas with others. I will not expect my moods to be only good or "positive vibes only." I owe myself the space to feel all my emotions, to process them all naturally. I am powerful enough to handle the entire gamut of emotions that this elegant life offers us. I allow them to come and to pass, I allow myself to process my emotions authentically and at the pace that feels most appropriate for me.

—Sylvester McNutt III

Affirm:

I Have Peace Of Mind

I am at peace with who I am today. I accept that I'd like to shift and improve things, but that improvement must come in time. Today I love who I am. I am happy with who I am, and I will allow any future developments to come naturally. I am in total alignment, and I trust that everything will come to me. Peace of mind is one of the greatest feelings, and I wake up with gratitude and acknowledgment for this space each day.

—Sylvester McNutt III

I like some of y'all, ha!

I feel good about the character of the people who are in my life. It's not about the number of people I have in my life; it's about the quality, and my people are the best. I am proud of the people I know, and I am grateful to have them in my life. Community is everything and I am in a gracious place when it comes to connections, relationships and community. I actually like some of y'all, ha!

—Sylvester McNutt III

Affirm:

I am going to focus on the good in life. I am going to focus on the positive. I am going to allow happiness to be the baseline emotion that I return to. I deserve to be happy, to feel good, and to create positive energy every day.

— Sylvester McNutt III

Affirm:

I have at least one person I can share ideas with. I have at least one person I can open up to. I have at least one person who gets me. Knowing this gives me peace of mind because having at least one person to share energy with is a blessing that I cannot take for granted.

—Sylvester McNutt III

Affirm:

I am worthy of genuine love—a love that isn't about tallies and scores. I deserve the love that gives freedom and healing, grows, and never destroys. I am worthy of this love from myself, from family, and in the form of partnership.

—Sylvester McNutt III

Affirm:

There are endless opportunities for me. I am doing the best with what I have, but if that doesn't work, I am okay mentally because I know there is something else out there for me. I believe in who I am and what I have to offer. I vibrate at the frequency of abundance, therefore, I never worry or fret. Success flows through my energy field every day.

—Sylvester McNutt III

Affirm:

I am grateful for all the small steps and victories I have accomplished. I remind myself to appreciate what I have completed. My list of accomplishments is far longer than I realize. I am going to take a few moments today to appreciate what I have done.

—Sylvester McNutt III

Success Is Recovery

I deserve to rest and to unwind peacefully. I deserve to heal and process life at my pace. I deserve to be free from unruly energy. I deserve to sleep with peace of mind and calmness. I am the kind of person who values healing, recovery, and restoration. I want my energy field to be balanced, therefore, I will push and grind but I will not violate my healing process. To me, success is about recovery and replenishing my energy.

—Sylvester McNutt III

Goodnight Affirmation

I release today's energy. I can and I will sleep peacefully. I have peace of mind because I know I am a good person. I do well, and I mean well by people. I release today because I know tomorrow will be bright and full of opportunity for me. I release today knowing I gave myself to the day, and the things that didn't work out for me today will teach me a lesson for tomorrow. I will sleep well because I deserve to.

—Sylvester McNutt III

Success Is Sleep

If you want to be successful then you should get a whole night of sleep tonight. If you want to be successful you should put the cellphone down and allow your natural melatonin to kick in. If you want to be successful then you should decompress each night and sleep peacefully. If you want your dream body, dream job or the dream relationship you need to go to sleep so you can restore and recovery.

—Sylvester McNutt III

Self-love

is about trying to get a whole night of sleep each night. If we want to have a serious conversation about self-love, then we also need to talk about sleep. Being sleep deprived is not love, it's not the way and anyone preaching that you should neglect sleep for goals doesn't give a damn about your life or vitality.

With love, go to bed.

-- Sylvester McNutt III

Affirm: I am worthy of celebrating my life. I deserve to win, to be happy, to be free. I deserve to love and to be loved. I deserve to have healthy people in my life. I deserve to see myself thrive and heal, and I won't settle for less than that.

—Sylvester McNutt III

I don't care what anyone says, your birthday is not just another day. Your birthday is a day to reflect, to honor your journey, and to find a deep gratitude that you are here. Use your birthday to celebrate yourself and your community. Use your birthday to come together, to laugh, to cry, to be seen and heard. Your birthday is not just another day!

—Sylvester McNutt III

Affirm:

I am grateful to see another year. Things change so fast that the future can become blurry. But at this moment, I am thankful for life. I am grateful for the big heart I have. I am proud of how far I've come. I am proud of what I have survived. I am confident that my life will move toward where it deserves to be, and I'm so grateful for the loving people who share their life with me.

—Sylvester McNutt III

I Release Everything That is Beneath Me

I am grateful that certain dramatic people and situations are beyond me now. I see and honor my growth, and I will not allow myself to participate in situations that do not move me forward. You're right, the older me might have engaged certain situations and people in a particular manner, but I am no longer that person — this is a new me now. I release everything that is beneath me now, including all older versions of me. I am free.

—Sylvester McNutt III

Affirm:

I am worthy of creating my vision.

No matter what I go through, I will repeatedly tell myself, "I am worthy." No matter what others think, I have to believe this for my life. I can do it if I set my mind to it and believe what's possible. Life is about your belief system and your habits, and I am in alignment with my vision. I am here to use my skills, my energy and my passions for a big reason. I claim this and I honor this realization with gratitude and genuine appreciation.

—Sylvester McNutt III

Affirm:

I am willing to leave spaces where I am unwanted. I do not need to fight and make my voice heard in places that do not want me. My only focus is to move to spaces where I am wanted and valued. I am worthy of these spaces. I am a magnet for these spaces.

—Sylvester McNutt III

Affirm:

I am worthy of leaving bad energy behind me. I am worthy of moving up and on so I can be freed from past stories. I am worthy of staying present with my focus. If lousy energy comes to me today, it will be repelled and rejected.

—Sylvester McNutt III

Affirm:

I will use my voice to be my own best friend at this moment and move forward. I will speak to myself in a kind and loving tone. I will offer myself compassion and grace as I go through this phase of life.

—Sylvester McNutt III

Affirm:

I am confident in the choices that I am making in life. Even if I am wrong or a lesson presents itself, that's okay. I am not here to be perfect or right all of the time. I am here to be human, and I embrace my humanity. I allow myself the grace to learn and to be a magnet for new experiences. I don't chase perfection, instead, I choose to accept that I am a magnet for everything I want in life.

Affirm:

I deserve to be around love that feels genuine and passionate. There is too much abundance in the world for anything less than this. I release anything that is less than love.

—Sylvester McNutt III

Affirm:

I deserve to be with someone who sees me as I am, but they challenge me to my depths so I may unfold into the most profound versions of my soul.
—Sylvester McNutt III

Affirm:

I am so happy that I choose actions that prolong the quality of my life. I am here to live a full life and to inspire others to show up for the life that they deserve. I try my best to choose a lifestyle that reflects self-love.

—Sylvester McNutt III

Affirm:

I am happy for my level of confidence, however, I love being a curious student of life. I will not pretend to have it all together, but I am grateful that I continue to move forward, ask questions, and keep learning along the way.

—Sylvester McNutt III

Self-Love Affirmations To Repeat Daily

I am human

I love myself

I accept myself

I am healing, daily

I am magnet for success

I nourish my relationships

I love the people in my life

I am grateful for my lessons

I am aligned with the life I deserve

—Sylvester McNutt III • Loving Yourself Properly

9

Choose Your Habits Wisely

I DELIVERED A LECTURE THIS MORNING ON THE new emotional wellness application Mine'd called "Small Habits," and the framework for it was aimed at how we can develop and become more conscious of the habits we have. I am one of the original creators of this app. You can find the app in your app store on your cellphone. We have therapists, authors, teachers, yoga teachers, human connection specialists and so many other teachers who hold space for transformation. Mine'D is a great resource and I'm proud to be one of the creators; join us.

When it comes to self-love I see a direct connection with our habits and how we view our lives. For some, we will need to break, change and release old habits. And for many of us tapping into self-love it will require us to learn, adapt and to practice new habits.

Habits matter because when we talk about self-love, essentially we are talking about what we choose over and over, which is nothing more than our habits. Therefore observing and, in some cases, shifting habits will change the potency we possess when it comes to loving ourselves properly. Without going any further—and without shame—we know right now the exact habits that are preventing us from moving into our deepest alignment, into our highest vibration, into the goals and desires that we are dreaming of.

Habits make up 40 percent of our unconscious behavior. Habits are our brain's way of increasing its efficiency. Having a newborn or young baby around you will help you see how the human brain develops habits in real time, and I must say that we are so incredible as a species. It was such an honor to be able to watch my little guy grow daily, to watch his brain compute and process his experience. Watching a child learn, experiment, and evolve is one of the richest experiences; and if we allow it, it can help us, as adults, relearn ourselves. Another rich experience is when we can bring objective awareness in and say, "Oh, so if I just shift this one thing a little bit here and this little thing over there, then I will completely change my life. Woah!"

I'll never forget the very first time my son felt wind; we were in Flagstaff, Arizona, at the lake. It was early summer, and the breeze from across the lake was cool but not cold. The rhythm of the wind felt calming to me, and as I looked at him, he was using all his power to focus on deep observation to what the wind was as it graced his face. He felt every second of the experience, allowing himself to become totally present. It was beautiful to watch Mason go through that and his mom, Daisy held him in place. She too, was lodged into the moment of observing his presence — it was one of our first memories that defined us as a little unit. He was not thinking about college, his next meal, or anything other than this moment. It reminded me to choose the present more often, to make a habit of staying present and not obsessing about where I am going. That moment brought me deep into my body, into alignment.

The first time you did something, it required a lot of your concentration and brainpower (like observing wind).

But as you repeatedly do a behavior, it becomes easier. The mental power you need to perform these tasks decrease significantly. This process is called "chunking," and it is the root of habits. Every day we rely on these "chunks" of behavior unconsciously to prepare our day. This, my friend, is why observing our habits is so crucial—it's one of the most important building blocks to the house of how we are living.

Since 40 percent of our behavior is unconscious through the form of habits. It seems intuitive to me that we, as students of life, must ask, *How do we become more conscious of our habits* and *how do we create new habits to bring our life into total alignment?*

"You are the master of your fate." This is a phrase that I do not take lightly. On my right inner arm, I have a tattoo that says, "Master of my fate." As we dive into any framework that addresses the concepts of habit, it is important that you adopt a growth mindset here. No matter what you have been through in life, at this point, you owe it to yourself to allow this to be the moment you will become the master of your fate. Regardless of past defeats, you must believe and say to yourself, "I can do this. I am the master of my fate."

Self-love is about your belief system. Choose to live in this moment and believe that you have the power to form new habits. Now, this is going to require sacrifice and chaos, yes plenty of chaos. You're going to have to stir things up in your life to get out of your bad habits. Welcome the chaos because the chaos is going to help you break the emotional bond to the thought or belief system that has kept you trapped, and no, breaking habits is not easy but it is necessary.

HOW LONG DOES IT TAKE TO FORM A HABIT?

Have you ever heard that forming a habit takes 21 days? I, too, used to think this until I did the research on forming habits. In 1960, Dr. Maxwell Maltz created a best-selling book called *Psycho-Cybernetics.* In that book, he was making a rather casual observation about his patients in that the observation was run with as a fact.

Maltz noted, "These, and many other commonly observed phenomena tend to show that it requires a minimum of about 21 days for an old mental image to dissolve and a new one to gel." He wasn't wrong with his assessment; it just wasn't interpreted correctly, but the media ran with it and—since we have heard it over and over—we accept it.

Here's the truth: we have to throw away the idea that habits get formed in 21 days. According to a 2009 study published in the *European Journal of Social Psychology*, it takes 18 to 254 days for a person to form a new habit.

For example, certain habits take longer to form, and some are easier. Also, forming a habit isn't a cookie-cutter concept; it varies based on what each person is capable of. It may only take me 18 days to get in the rhythm of working out after a month off, and it may take you 254 days or more. Because of this, it's crucial to our mental health that we offer ourselves compassion as we tackle the concept of changing or eliminating habits. Let's not force a timeline of expectation of these behaviors, but instead, let's use this information to help increase our self-awareness and also to be pragmatic.

Many people don't reach certain goals simply because their expectation of when they occur isn't pragmatic, and the effort that is needed to create a new habit while allowing the old one to perish is not appropriately granted. In the frame of working out, it may or may not be realistic for you to say, "Hey, I have not done physical fitness in ten years, but because it's my New Year's resolution, I am going to start going 6 days a week." The truth is you need a plan that is going to get you in there at least 3 days a week while you focus on changing sleep, hydration, belief system, and eating habits. Most people think working out is the key to getting in shape when it's actually a multitude of habits that all need to work in congruence with one another. Another reason we don't create what we want is that we fail to recognize that there's more than one habit that needs to change.

No, we are not shooting down lofty goals because they can serve us if we can execute them; instead we are developing a framework for longevity and sustainability, which to me is way more important. It's about setting small routines that compound; that's the sweet spot. That is what

Loving Yourself Properly is all about. As you read this book and begin to take action, it's important that you go into new behaviors, goals, and ideas with the right target and with self-compassion.

It's important that you grieve old habits and acknowledge them. This process makes building new habits even easier. On the soul level, when you allow yourself to become present, to honor a habit that you now have, and then to consciously speak into the world that you are breaking this habit, it becomes more powerful for your brain. This increases the odds that you will stick with it.

THINGS CHANGE

August 2019 was a tough month for me. I had a great birthday celebration with Daisy in Los Angeles on the twenty-third, and then my life changed that week. I tore my groin on the twenty-seventh, and honestly that injury changed my life. There was a deep butterfly effect from the injury that permeated all the way into 2020, and then in 2020 my son was born and a pandemic hit the world. That is the reason why it took me so long to finish this book, because honestly, I was trying to process and heal my own life.

I was working out six days a week before, and once the accident happened, I kept eating like I was working out as frequently. I also celebrated the fact that I was going to be a father by having wine multiple times a week, probably too much if we are being honest. I put myself in a situation where I stopped moving, became sedentary because of the injury and used alcohol to cope and to celebrate. I kept my calories the same and even added more; plus there was the impending stress of shifting my life around to prepare for fatherhood. Before I knew it, I went from ripped and muscular to having an extra thirty pounds of body fat that brought new challenges, pain, and disadvantages. The extra thirty pounds that I was carrying slowly began to erode my confidence and self-image. I share this, vulnerably because I know the truth in these stories can connect with you and serve you. My habits changed, and I was not fully aware of them until I didn't recognize my body anymore.

When I finally came back to my senses, I knew exactly what I needed to do. I was finally cleared by my doctor and went back to the gym.

I went to the infrared sauna before my first workout, and I sat in there for forty-five minutes. I did a deep meditation in there with no phone, no music, just my breath and the heat. I said affirmations and words of encouragement to my body. I knew that I needed a healing ritual with my body so I could let it know that the thirty pounds had to go.

I grabbed the excess fat that was around my belly not with contempt, not with shame, not with hate, but I held it. I said aloud, "Thank you for allowing me to experience what you gave me. Dear body, thank you for keeping me alive, thank you for allowing me to recover from my injury. Thank you for showing me that I was neglecting you by not stretching and getting my loose. Thank you for showing me that I was being too hard on my joints. Thank you for showing me that I needed a better recovery routine. Dear mind, thank you for staying sharp as you can be." And I rubbed my belly and just connected with my breath and my body. I told the excess fat cells in my body that it was time for them to go now, I honored them, I thanked them, and I told them that a new body was coming.

I had to choose self-love, even with the things I wanted to change. I had to change my habits by preparing food and being conscious of my portion sizes, reprioritizing my sleeping habits of going to bed at the same time, recommitting to training in the gym. I agreed to recommit to making working out about fun and community, and sharing my goals with the people I loved and asking for their support. Also, I had to stop drinking alcohol. I had give up alcohol for all of the reasons. It's a shitty tool to use to cope, it gives you calories that are useless, it costs money, and it lowers your energetic vibration.

As a result, I lost the thirty pounds and now have a body that I love, but it's not because I hated the old body—no. I found love for the old body, and that day in the sauna was a grief ritual. It allowed me to allow an old version of me to die. I did not allow shame to come into that room because shame does not live here. I went into the shame wound and decided that I was only going to use positive affirmations and positive words to do away with an old version of me.

If you struggle in figuring out what habits you need to change, ask your community to support you in the introspection, but do so without shame. Ask three to five friends to write to you about some habits that you can change, tell them to be brutally honest, and tell them that you want to read those letters with them together. I strongly believe that you should be making your goals based on what you need; however, there is power by asking your husband, wife, kids, or family, "What's one habit I could work on that will make all our lives better? Any ideas?" This practice also brings you into deeper intimacy with your loved ones because it can lead to a conversation about wants and needs. If you do this, they'll be able to see you, hold you, and acknowledge you on your journey. That can stand as a grief ritual.

When you finish this book, I want you to become extremely aware of your habits (without shame). And once you do, then you can make the shifts. Without honest self-awareness, there is no point in talking about habits because you will simply lie and say you aren't the problem. You, as a human are not the problem, but in the name of self-love we each may have habits that may be destructive, and therefore, it is at least worth introspecting.

With compassion, you got this.

The Three-Step Loop of Habits

- Cue
- Routine
- Reward

Let's discuss,

If you can see or hear these words today, that means you have the power to shift harmful habits. To do that, though, an understanding of how they form will solidify your confidence even further. This isn't about shame or putting yourself down; most people have habits that they want to shift, especially if that will bring them a more resonant quality of life.

The 1990s was a great time for TV. My favorites were *Martin*, *Fresh Prince*, *Home Improvement*, and *Power Rangers*. I had a habit of watching TV upon finishing my homework, especially during Chicago's winters. I was not thrilled to go play in the frozen tundra. Ha! The '90s weren't just about quality TV either. A group of researchers from Massachusetts Institute of Technology discovered the neurological process at the core of every habit—cue, routine, and reward. This research changed the foundational way we observed and talked about habits.

When we are working with self-love and trying to make changes in our lives, our habits are a crucial component of the equation. In fact, I will even argue that without an examination our habits, we will never begin to gain enough momentum toward loving ourselves properly.

Cue is any trigger that tells your brain when and which habit to use.

Routine is an activity, emotion, or behavior.

Reward is how your mind determines if a loop is beneficial to you or not.

The cue and the reward have a powerful influence in creating habits. They're the cause of cravings and make you repeat behaviors or actions. Speaking of TV, how many times have you been watching a show when a sexy food commercial comes on, and then you say, "Oh yeah, I need to order exactly what I just saw"? That commercial and those marketers behind it are trying to *cue* you to order their food. If you order the food on your phone or computer, eat, and feel good, you will order again. They are prying on how our brain is wired. They **cue** us with the commercial; we desire their food. Our **routine** is to order their food, and then we are **rewarded** because we feel good while we eat it. These marketers know this and they prime us because we don't know it.

Last week the NFL season started. It's a social norm and expectation that you go to the bar and get loud, eat a bunch of fried food, and drink beer—even past your boundaries because our society has embraced drinking, even though it's bluntly toxic the way we go about it. In the football context, the social norms trigger our habits—excessive drinking, loudness and rottenness, and even barbaric rudeness all under the muse of being a fanatic of a team.

The bartender will look at you crazily when you say that you do not want any beer during a football game. If you opt for a salad instead of the wings, people will think you're strange. And this societal pressure is baked into our different frameworks, families, and communities. Personally,

I think this society is crazy for promoting a toxic lifestyle but that's my opinion which is why I strongly believe in trying to live a life based in holistic health. Change the story if you will, but the same framework operates under different names.

This is why you have to be the master of your own fate—you get to choose what your life is and is not. You do not have to drink alcohol because everyone is; you do not have to eat unhealthily because that is what is socially acceptable in a certain environment. You have the right to create and reinforce new habits regardless of what everyone else is doing.

You should only get beer if you genuinely want to, if you are self-aware enough to know that you are making a choice. You should only get fried food and eat over your caloric threshold if you consciously are choosing that without shame. Many of us are not concisely choosing, and many of us use shame to cope, to succumb to pressures. I know this is tough work, but it's the only option that gives peace of mind and that is sustainable.

To simply ask, "What am I choosing right now and why?" you'll be choosing your voice, you'll be choosing what's best for your body, and your choices will be authentic. Always ask yourself, "Is this decision a loving decision?" and trust the answer that comes. Your body will not lie to you.

This process is simply one of deep introspection, and it's vital to your success. You may be on a fitness journey where you are trying to reclaim power in your life, and if so, then alcohol is not going to help you—at least this was the conclusion that I eventually reached for my own journey; it may not apply to you. When I was looking at the equation of self-love, I knew that there was something I had to subtract to get everything I wanted—empty carbs, added sugar, lower inhibitions, and lack of appetite control sound like a disaster if you are trying to get yourself healthy. The reward of feeling better, looking better, and having a better quality of life needs to be the driver, the motivational pull that you hold on to. Again, that was my journey — you can change the specific story details to match your path.

When you have two desires that go against each other, they are called competing desires. Competing desires have the ability to destroy your habits or the ability to support you in forging new habits. In the name of self-love, in the name of gaining confidence and control, pick the desires that you want the most so they don't have to compete. Stick to the habits that will help you toward that desire. This, again, may not be completed when you are alone, and you must ask your community to support you. Make a declaration about what you want and what you deserve, not what instantly feels good. Think long term here, think sustainability and vitality.

I couldn't find the originator of this phrase, but we've all used it. "Willpower is not a muscle, but it is a skill." I love the sentiment because that tells us that the more we use it, the stronger it gets. Changing habits is not just about willpower, but it is ultimately about knowing how they work. Now that we know how they work, our willpower should increase, and that is the catalyst for the change we desire.

Using self-awareness to examine our habit loops, for most of us, this practice will be the key to freedom. In Charles Duhigg's *The Power of Habit: Why We Do What We Do in Life and Business*, he says that the first step in changing a habit is to become aware of the routine and then experiment with rewards, isolate the cue, and finally have a plan.

Let's use our football, beer, and wings combination to dive a little deeper. I want to make sure you have a practical example of this in case you need to break it down; plus this is a situation that affected the younger me deeply since I grew up with two alcoholic parents.

I like talking about alcohol, sobriety, and the relationship with such because it seems like this society keeps this conversation out of the frame. Please note that I am not trying to create shame, call anyone names, or vilify either of the three choices—drinking beer, eating wings, or watching sports. My only intention is to to name the space so we can recognize similar spaces in our own life, so we can be aware, and then so we can choose.

However, when you have a country like the United States that has a 40+ percent obesity metric in 2020, it's fair to say that people need to start examining habits (my hope is that *Loving Yourself Properly* may facilitate a safe space to explore that conversation and others that relate). And more importantly to me, it seems like we have a system that needs to be destroyed (many of them, if you will), and I am all for destroying systems, especially if the system is holding us back from our highest self. It calls for a shift in awareness to destroy destructive systems.

A Practical Introspective Examination

Awareness—The reason we are drinking beer in excess at football games is that the culture promotes partying, drinking, and binge eating. It promotes sitting down for three hours and overconsuming until the game is over, which can last for three hours or more.

Often we sit for much longer to watch multiple games. Football offers an opportunity for family and friends to get together, which is a great benefit that many of us want since we tend to live *busy* lives. (Please mentally substitute *football* with something else that fits the narrative of your life such as Sunday Funday brunches, binge drinking on Fridays or Saturdays, soccer matches, or just an *I'm off work, and it's time to drink, rageeeeeee-party-time, ha!*)

Next you'll have to do some introspection with some less obvious questions. What's the cue for this routine? Is it hunger? Boredom? Low blood sugar? Peer pressure? Wanting to fit in? And what's the reward? The excess drinking itself? Seeing people? Being in a place where you can yell and scream and it is okay? The temporary distraction from life? Dating and meeting people at the bar who may be love interests? Do you just really enjoy wings? To figure this out, you'll need to experiment and allow yourself to become fully aware. And again we are not vilifying anything or introducing shame—no, we are becoming aware. That's it.

Charles then recommends experimenting with rewards. Rewards are powerful because they satisfy cravings. To figure out which cravings are driving particular habits, it's useful to experiment with different rewards. In our sports and drinking situation, you could try to go to a football meeting and not have wings and beer; and then the next week, you'll have wings and beer. You could try to watch the game alone and see what cravings and impulses you have. It's all about gathering data, as a sovereign scientist of self.

I recommend using a journal and recording your thoughts, feelings, and observations. You may observe that you feel no difference; you may feel better or worse—it's about your own experience and observation. The purpose of the experiment is to get to the root of what you are craving, what your true desire is.

Once you get to the root, then you can make a plan and intention for how you want to attack things. It's not about shame, vilifying any behavior, or putting yourself down. It's only about allowing yourself the space to compassionately become a scientist, to experiment—to get the information you need to forge new habits.

And yes, I brought up football, but please change it to fit your narrative. This will require that you ask questions with the intent of total observation. You should do this now.

Setting a Clear Intention: The Path to Your Next Level

First, the most important thing to focus on is *the why*. Changing in the name of health, survival, and quality of life seems to be one of the most powerful, transformative tools out there. Changing for the betterment of your child or children or relationship is extremely important, and it also has some great transformative power behind it. Whenever you want to make a change in your life, you must start with the why. The why—a clearly defined reason or idea—helps you focus. The why creates an opportunity to instill discipline and consistency into your day-to-day habits. The why propels you forward. The why gives you clarity about what mindsets and behaviors are needed—find the why and be patient as you do so. Your why may be grand, or it may be minor, but all whys matter.

Second, when attempting to change, you have to ask, *What or who is going to hold me back from my why or the goal I seek?* We all have something that is holding us back, consciously or unconsciously, and we have to ask that question to try to bring it to our awareness. This may not be easy, and it may not occur overnight. Even still, you have to ask, and you must allow those answers to find you at the pace in which they need to.

A practical example of this is the mom who wants to find more alone time so she can do the self-care routine that is going to give her longevity, a situation I have total compassion for because I know how hard it can be as a parent to get away, but we both know that our duty is to show up as our most potent selves. We cannot neglect our self-care, so our work is to figure out how to teach and show our kids why self-care is important. So for that mom, she has to ask, "What is stopping me, and how do I make space for what is needed?"

Last, you need to make goals. Without making goals, you will not be able to see your progress, but I have a trick for you with the goals. *Don't make your goals solely based on a metric; make your goal behavior based. A behavior-based goal may include a metric, but its existence is to drive behavior, which in turn will create an outcome. Behavior-based goals create lifestyles and metric based goals create temporary moments of satisfaction. Please, never forget this: make behavior-based goals because we are after an aligned life.*

So let's go back to the person who is focusing on weight loss. If you set a goal of "I want to lose forty pounds," how do we know if this is even the right target? Who the hell made up forty pounds of all the numbers? Is that your high school target weight you're setting here? Hmm, I wonder.

That's a metric-based goal, and I'm not saying it's not possible; I'm saying there's a more compassionate way that will give you better results. Instead of metrics, use behavior by saying, "My goal is to train at least four days a week with my trainer and to keep a food journal so I can consistently monitor what I am eating while keep self-compassion at the forefront of my ways. My goal is to not use shame when I eat, to gain knowledge on how my body responds to certain foods." The four-day-a-week-training and food journal plan is behavior based and is driving an action. It's those actions that will create the results of potentially losing the forty pounds. Does this register with you?

Another thing I love about behavior-based goals is that they can be used forever. I am after the longevity game, the game of holistic health and healing — you are too. The goal of losing forty pounds is a temporary game; once you do it, then what? If the goals are behavior driven with the understanding that behavior drives results, then we are inviting ourselves to the sweet spot.

Without that physical representation, your success may feel like you have not accomplished anything, and you give up too soon. Your goals should be specific and should also include the behaviors you are using to get toward the goals. Researchers have shown that when we train our minds to think about what we desire in life and strive toward attaining it, the mind automatically rewires itself to obtain the ideal self-image and makes it an essential part of our identity. If we accomplish the goal, we produce fulfillment; and if we don't, our brain continues pushing us until we reach it.

If you want to change yourself for the better, you will have to start with your habits. We talked about the framework of how to change a habit. Then you will have to find the why, a reason, a purpose because that motivating factor is what will allow you to stay committed. Once you feel like you have a purpose, it drives your willpower and discipline, and that is the formula for using goals and habits to shift your life toward the direction you want to flow.

If you had a vision for it, then that is your proof that it is possible. Break up with the people, behaviors and the environments that will prevent you from making it happen. The second that you decide to let go the universe will conspire to reward you. Your body will signal your DNA to align with that vision. Always believe in your vision and let go so you have the hands, the energy and the capacity to hold it. It's coming; claim it!

—Sylvester McNutt III

Your life is about what you choose and who you choose over and over. Be mindful of where you put your time, what beliefs you choose to follow, and what habits you repeat. The majority of your life's outcome exists right between these sweet spots.

—Sylvester McNutt III

Making excuses about what you don't have or what you cannot do is no longer the vibration for us. Instead, let's look at our bad habits and begin to work on them — without shame. The next level will come the day that we get control over our bad habits. Why, because once we focus on those bad habits we break those energetic bonds, and once we break those then we have more clarity and energy to use towards our purpose. We'll feel a transition as we gain more power and more love, and we'll feel lighter.

—Sylvester McNutt III

All you have is time and energy. Investigate how you're using them, where they're going, and who gets them from you. Do not support habits that result in you wasting your energy or your time. Those resources are too valuable to waste. Choose wisely.

—Sylvester McNutt III

Invest your time in your community, in your healing, in habits that give you the life you deserve. Every day is a new day to choose habits that bring you deeper into love and purpose. It's also an opportunity to drop habits that kill you slowly. Choose wisely, and please choose the habits that are going to give you a high quality of life and longevity. Claim this energy for you!

—Sylvester McNutt III

Stop doing dumb shit just because people around you do it. That's not an excuse that you can accept anymore. The game of self-love even means choosing the opposite of what everyone else is doing. Save yourself, break up with those poor habits, and put all your energy into your vitality, healing, and passions—that's the sweet spot. Claim this!

--Sylvester McNutt III

There is

an immense amount of power inside you, and the only thing holding you back is the belief system that keeps you married to bad habits. Once you choose to divorce that belief system, you will notice how much freedom you have, how much power you have. It's not the habits that are causing the biggest problem; it's the belief system—let it go. Just by seeing these words, please recognize that your soul is a magnet for freedom. You are already free.

—Sylvester McNutt III

Sometimes we go two steps forward, and then we take four steps back. This feeling sucks. The main reason it happens is that we fall back into certain bad habits, and we continue to support the belief system that supports them. If this is you, then you need support — so drop your ego and ask for help. Friends, coaches, trainers, therapists, the community, and everyone in your life are here to help you. You must ask them to support you; tell them what you need. And then doing this work will be ten times easier. You can do this, together.

—Sylvester McNutt III

Be loving

and compassionate toward yourself as you work on bringing new habits into your life. You don't have to build a house in a day. You don't need to make millions overnight. You don't have to change your body composition in one day. No matter what your goal or dream is, just note two things: first, it's possible; and second, it's okay to take slow steps daily as you build new, loving habits.

—Sylvester McNutt III

No matter where you are in life, the number one habit you can add is having more self-compassion. That means no more beating yourself up—only encouraging vibes, words, and connections. Be your best friend and be a dear friend to others. We don't need anymore bullies around. Claim the love that is vibrating inside of you.

—Sylvester McNutt III

10

IGNITE THE FIRE:

AN OPEN LETTER

March 5, 2021
An Open Letter

"I Came Here to Ignite The Fire In My Soul"

I didn't come to this world to be dull, die with all my thoughts and ideas, and not fully participate in life. I didn't come here to do jobs that I hate, to pretend to entertain people who despise me, to walk through life using an inefficient state of mind. I do not want to appease people who make me feel small to gain a false sense of approval. I am not here to be liked or hated; in fact, that external validation is not my mission. While I certainly need and crave love, I will only accept genuine love from people who know how to create a container of safety for our experiences.

I came here for engagement and experience. I came here for love, connection and to play. I came here to learn, to ask questions, to expand my mind. I came here to experience the experience of life, fully. I came here to ignite my passions on fire and pursue them.

I didn't come here to avoid the tough conversations that build intimacy and connection. I want them, no matter how arduous and deep they are. I didn't come here to do relationships that leave me curious about where we stand. I do not have any desire to hold grudges, to be right, to yell and scream with anyone. I do not have the desire to do life on autopilot. I didn't come here to wake up to an alarm that I hate, sit in rush hour traffic, and simply pay bills. There is so much more in life that I need, want, and am worthy of.

"What is that?" you ask. I want to sip coffee in the mornings not because I am in a rush but because I want to feel the robustness of the flavors as they meander through my body. I want to become so present that I can daydream about where that coffee bean came from and the conditions that helped create such a wonderful flavor.

I want to sit outside and feel the wind as it wraps around my body, as I feel my ancestors' voices tell me to keep going, to keep persevering and endeavoring. My ancestors lived and died to better their lives and those of the people who came after them. I am one of those people, and I am indebted to them. I want to honor their steps, sacrifices, and embraces with my life. I want to love myself so deeply that they become proud and feel like their steps were worth it, and I want to keep walking miles that matter for them — and for those who will follow after me.

I want to eat fresh, nutrient-dense food. Food that has earthly flavors and is full of soul and life. I will not settle for less than this. I will not settle for what is easy because I love my body, and I want nutrient-dense whole foods to enter my vessel. I want to check in with my body and see how it is doing. If it needs more protein, water, fats, or carbohydrates, then I will give it what it needs to be rich. I want to honor every meal I come across while taking a second to acknowledge the meal, the farmer, the animals, the earth, the people who have helped make this moment happen. I want to feel the richness of sweet, savory, and sour foods as they conglomerate together to create explosions in my body.

I came here to get a full night of sleep as often as possible, to honor my body and rest, and to allow each night to matter as the night brings healing and restoration to my body. The rituals around sleeping, calming the body, and creating a healthy sleep space must be appreciated and honored. I came here to make my sleep routine one of the most essential practices in my life. I know that self-love is about sleep, and sleep is not something I want to neglect ever again. I bought into the hustle and bustle, the "stay busy and die" mindset that society gave us, but I reject that now. Hustle is not more important than sleep.

I want to have the strength and power to persuade people to value their sleep ten times more than they ever had before, for we live in a society that wants us to live like zombies. I want you, my lover, my kids, my friends, my family, to realize that loving yourself properly means getting in bed and honoring the restorative healing that sleep brings.

I am a nerd, and I need to learn. I need to explore. I need to ask questions. I don't have to know it all, but I do care about staying curious because that curiosity charges me up. I want to know how people feel, what they think.

I came here to ask the burning questions that everyone else is afraid of — I am not scared of the backlash of asking an inappropriate question. I don't mind if I am cancelled by others, for as long as I accept and love myself then I have already won in life. They told us talking about money is taboo, and most people don't have financial literacy, so no, I cannot accept that. I need to know about your financial understanding and situation, and you can learn about mine.

We can teach each other and grow. Can I help you get paid? Can I put you in a position to take care of your family? If so, I must do it. You might know someone I need to know, and if you can introduce us, please do. They tell us not to talk about money, but one of the leading causes of divorce is financial troubles. Where is the common sense in this? A lack of funds creates stress because we need money to access specific resources, experiences, and safety elements. I want us all to be rich and I won't back down until we all "make it".

It sounds like we need to have healthy conversations about money, about our connection to it, about how we can develop stronger habits that bring understanding to our relationships. This is why we have to invite conversations about money and wealth because that, too, is self-love, especially since the current society requires us to have it to access what we need to survive. Many of us buy things to fill an emotional void, and that has to stop. I challenge you to be totally conscious of how you're spending your money.

I came here to ask my friends to show up fully in their lives. I don't want to see you sell yourself short, I don't want to see you in pain, I don't want to see you settling for situations that are beneath you. I want you to win. I want to get in the trenches to fight with you—but you have to want that for yourself too. You are worth fighting for — so fight, dammit. And after you've fought, relax and recover.

I want you to fight for your life—no more gray area, no more being afraid to speak up on how you feel. I want you to fight for what you deserve. Don't settle for the bare minimum from yourself. Why do that? Maybe it's because of outdated thinking, but now we don't use shame, guilt, or fear to stop us. We don't bypass either; we make space for all of the things—we acknowledge everything alone, if you need it, or together, if you need it, and we must fight for the life you deserve. I didn't come here to play with my life. So, my friend, I have to hold you to a high standard.

You came here to ignite the fire in your soul. To start a fire, you need material, friction, and the right environment—that's it. You have plenty of material for your life. You have a beautiful life story; you've been through the darkness, and you are still here with a deep soul and whole heart. You've brought richness and love to as many people as you can. You've committed and even overcommitted, and that's great. Now it's your turn.

You have enough to give, and you are worthy of receiving love—believe that. And now the *Loving Yourself Properly* journey wants to know this from you: what do you need to do so you can ignite your life, so you can put your soul in a place that feels like home? And even if you aren't home, the wanderlust that lives in your veins is strong enough to keep you in a place of safety as you travel around this majestic earth.

You came here to ignite your soul on fire, and the time is now. Allow yourself to play more and to get serious about what you need—both can be true at the same time. Allow yourself to love fully and to be loved fully. You are allowed to use deep gratitude to recognize how grateful you are for your body, for your spirit, for the people you know. Use gratitude to bring a boatload of acceptance and present joy to this life you have today.

You are allowed to sing songs that make you feel like you're on stage in front of eighty-thousand people. You're allowed to randomly drop that freestyle rap that comes to your brain when you're eating your favorite ice cream. If a joke is told and you have to cry because it's so funny, allow your body to lose control and your tears to fall. You came here to ignite life, to ignite your soul, to see the beauty in this experience.

In the coming days, you will feel a passion brewing. You will feel your soul burning, and that energy has to be used. You have to burn that energy. Cook any pain you have; burn it all away in this new vessel of life that you've created. You must cook any shame, fear, or low vibrational energy that is holding you back.

Allow this burning to singe the earth, to make a difference, to allow you to exude confident and positive energy, not because it's fake but because that is who you are, because you are unleashing yourself into this world. We need you to operate at your highest, at your most potent power. We need you to be flexible, agile, strong, and sharp. We need you to see the beauty in life, to play, to stay present, and to cherish every single moment.

11

THE GIFT OF SELF-COMPASSION

Self-Compassion Affirmations

I love my body
I love my mind
I love the life that I live
I love how I am growing
I am not afraid of change
I only aspire to be myself
I accept my past for what it is
I am so grateful to be here today
— Sylvester McNutt III

If you ever feel stuck between two choices, choose the one that feels like **self-love.** Choose the one that feels like you will be choosing self-compassion.

— Sylvester McNutt III

"Is this decision me loving myself properly?" Keep it simple, and whenever you feel stuck, use self-compassion to ask yourself this question. It will always bring you the truth.

— Sylvester McNutt III

As you begin to decide what you want to do with life, please do everything with love. Commit to releasing everything less than love. Commit to loving yourself properly with your nutrition choices, sleep patterns, and the relationships that you are choosing. There is a deep love that is flowing through your soul. I hope you tap into that love every day, and I hope you select choices that add to your vitality. You are already free — you are love.

— Sylvester McNutt III

The entire

world around you will respond and react to the way you love yourself. Treat yourself well and warm, and always do your best to choose the most loving way. When you make a mistake, be kind and offer yourself and those impacted an apology if needed. A self-apology can go a long way. Remember, the world will respond to your inner feelings and your external actions — choose wisely.

— Sylvester McNutt III

Throw away any idea of the concept of reaching perfection — it's not real. The path of perfection does not hold enough space for compassion, and as a human, we need genuine compassion and not the unrealistic chase of perfection. Fall in love with the concept of being consistent and patient as you work towards what matters most to you.

-- Sylvester McNutt III

Remember: **self-compassion** and **self-care** do not equate to being selfish. You can be warm and forgiving towards yourself. You're allowed to give yourself understanding. Take the time you need to cultivate true healing for yourself.
— Sylvester McNutt III

Dear Inner Critic,

You no longer have a spot on my roster. I'm choosing to cut you from this team. To create the championship pedigree, we must release all the energy that holds us back from our highest vibration. Therefore, the inner-critic will be released today. I'm choosing self-compassion and higher vibrations. I'm choosing the best me, which means the inner critic voice can no longer be here.

— Sylvester McNutt III

Essential Steps To Practice Self-Compassion

- **Genuine Self-Forgiveness**: take time to forgive yourself for mistakes, for poor behavior, and for your participation in events that do not match your present-day integrity. We all make mistakes. Find forgiveness; you deserve it.

- **Express Gratitude Daily**: use your journal, make a video, share it with a friend, do it during prayer or meditation. Or, you can keep it to yourself if you'd like it to be private and personal. Integrate a daily ritual to find gratitude for your mind, body, and existence.

- **Community Compassion Practice**: when you hear people you love beating themselves up or turning to unfriendly ways of talking, show up for them as support. Remind them of the self-compassion that they deserve. Supporting another in this manner helps you and them; and it makes the community more potent and aware.

— Sylvester McNutt III • Loving Yourself Properly

Self-Forgiveness Affirmations

I forgive myself.

I'm worthy of genuine forgiveness.

I am not the mistake(s) that I have made.

I'm worthy of forgiving myself for that mistake.

I'm worthy of forgiving myself for those mistakes.

I deserve to let go of the emotional weight that has held me back.

I made a mistake and that has caused me to upgrade my integrity. I'm thankful for the new integrity, and, I forgive my past versions.

I deserve to let go of the guilt that I have held on to for too long. Today, I release that guilt and all the emotional baggage that comes with it. I deserve forgiveness too. I deserve healing and compassion.

SELF-COMPASSION IS ONE OF THE GREATEST GIFTS that you will ever receive, a gift that can grow a garden of love, one that can nourish you through all your days, no matter how dark or bright.

This chapter is an invitation to use self-compassion as your baseline. If you have consumed this entire book, then I have to assume that you are already in the practice of offering yourself compassion, love, patience. Please take a second to honor yourself, to thank yourself, to thank the people in your community who have made space for you — woah, what a blessing to recognize. The very act of reading this book is an act of self-compassion. A book, that hopefully, was safe for you, a book that called you up, and reminded you of the deep love that lives inside of you.

Think about your favorite character in a book or show that you have obsessed over. Who comes to mind? When I was in college, a show called *Prison Break* featured a distinct character named Michael Scofield, who captivated my attention. I also loved how it was filmed in places that I knew about, like Chicago and Aurora, Illinois. Actor Wentworth Miller portrayed him, and author Paul Scheuring wrote the polarizing character. Executive producer Dawn Parouse was the person who created the idea for this character.

A murder conviction against his brother drove Scofield to save him from the death penalty. He assumed that his brother Lincoln did not do the murder; Lincoln Burrows, played by Dominic Purcell, was a tough but compassionate man who was in the wrong place at the wrong time. He didn't actually do the murder, and Scofield knew without any evidence that his brother wasn't capable of murdering someone.

The opening scene gives us a glimpse into Scofield's personality. It's midafternoon at Savings Bank, and seven or so customers are all lying facedown on the ground in terror. Two subdued security guards lay five feet from Michael as he holds a gun into the air, firing three shots. He then points at the manager and says, "The vault, open it."

The manager responds, "We can't. The branch manager isn't here. It's lunchtime. He's at White Castle."

Scofield repeats, "White Castle." As he smirks, the sound of a police helicopter and sirens looms closer. That glimpse into his sense of humor when fear usually will surmount struck me. And then they cue the dramatic, anxiety-driven music that subconsciously gets us hooked to the show.

The dread of being arrested and going to prison is a terrifying idea. Thousands of souls have perished in jail; it's uncomfortable and seems like an unfortunate occurrence. Scofield does not resist arrest, he doesn't smile or emote at all, and he doesn't react—as if he is where he wants to be. He is remarkably calm and poised. There is something about a bank robber and calmness that doesn't seem to go together.

As we dive deeper into the plot, we learn that Scofield has committed the crime to break his brother out of prison. Once we understand that the sole purpose of the story is so that Scofield can break Burrows out of the Illinois prison, our opinion of Scofield changes quickly. I love Scofield's existence because he makes us think in a dualistic way. We know right from wrong, yet Scofield makes us cheer for his flawed actions, even though he has good intentions—an intriguing duality.

A perfect example of this is that he is a nice guy and kind to everyone, even in prison. However, he manipulates the warden and eventually holds him at knifepoint so he and his brother can escape. Again he didn't want to do this, but it was necessary to save his brother's life.

As I meandered through this show, I kept asking myself, "Why am I cheering for this criminal? He committed a B and E (breaking and entering crime), held the warden at knifepoint, escaped prison, evaded authorities, and aided and abetted multiple criminals in leaving prison with him the night he and his brother broke out."

In one scene, he manipulated and took advantage of a mentally disabled person named Haywire and even helped a pedophile named Teabag escape, although the pedophile was going to alert the authorities to the escape plan, so in a way, Scofield had no choice. I screamed at the show in college, "Mike, you better not help Teabag! Leave his ass in there! Leave him in there!" I screamed at the top of my lungs.

If I told you that a real human being did this, you would scoff at the idea of liking this person, and you'd question my sanity. And if you told me you liked someone like this, I'd seriously wonder why. But that's the beauty of fiction; it exists to create thought and reflection and, of course, for just pure entertainment.

However, Scofield is not doing these just because he is bored or even because he is an evil and malicious person—no, not at all. Scofield has taken these extreme measures for love, for the family—he acts this way because he is putting his brother's life above his. Burrows has been framed, and they both know it. Scofield has given up a great experience to do these selfless acts.

He was a good-looking bachelor living in Chicago, Illinois. He graduated magna cum laude with a bachelor of science degree and a master of science degree in civil engineering from Loyola University Chicago. He became successful as a structural engineer at the prestigious architectural firm of Middleton, Maxwell, and Schaum in Downtown Chicago. Scofield had a "perfect life," and he threw it all away under the muse of helping his brother escape the death penalty.

And that was why I and millions of others became obsessed with this show and the characters. The writing, the drama, and the emotions ran wild throughout every episode. The show was written so well that it made us forget crimes were happening because the only thing we care about was an innocent life being saved.

And we justified terrible things happening to bad people as long as we could somehow free the people who were framed. We, as an audience, had an attachment to their outcome. And as each episode gave us flashbacks that detailed Scofield's childhood, we learned about the abandonment and abuse he suffered, which brought us into a frame that was purely empathetic. We began to grow fond of him. He had no sense of self-worth as a result of the trauma he went through. With low latent inhibition, he was very attuned to all the suffering around him. He was an empath, signaling that he was very empathic and sensitive to others' lives, feelings, and outcomes. Come on now, you can't hate an empath—you just can't do it.

As a consequence of being incapable of setting healthy boundaries with other people's suffering, he is extremely empathetic and altruistic toward other people's emotions. His sacrifices are not driven by self-worth, ego, or his own benefit. He lives to serve others—he is more concerned with other people's welfare than his own.

At this point, one of the most profound things happens to us as we meet this story in our consciousness. One of the most powerful emotions we experience seems to take over, and that is compassion. We begin to feel a deep-seated compassion for Scofield. We want his suffering to stop, we want his pain to go away, we want the right people to find out that his brother has been framed so the family can be granted clemency. Deep in our hearts, we offer him our deepest compassion and love. We want to hold him, nurture him and give him a hug.

I propose a question to think about, and maybe this question, if answered thoughtfully, can change the way you see yourself. Why is it that we fall in love with flawed characters, fictional and real? Why is it that we forgive these characters for their flaws, mostly if they mean well? Why is it that we can cheer for them when everything goes wrong in their life? Why is it that we cry, scream, and yell for these characters? The question of the day is, what would happen to our lives if we offered ourselves the full array of compassion that we offered so many other people who entered our lives? What would happen? I wonder.

When we think about these characters that we adore, we fall in love with their past. We look at their history and do not assume or take on their pain; we empathize with them. I challenge you to offer yourself compassion as you think of, recall, and relive your story.

Will Storr, the author of *The Science of Storytelling*, says, "Our sense of who we are depends, in significant part, on our memories." He makes a bold claim as he explains the parallels between characters we love and, from a science perspective, who we are as humans. In *The Science of Storytelling*, he says, "We're all fictional characters. We're the partial, biased, stubborn creations of our minds. To help us feel in control of the outside world, our brains lull us into believing things that aren't true among the most powerful of those beliefs, our sense of moral superiority."

Are we that much different from fictional characters? Don't we have past villains, drama in each one of our episodes, and the desire to overcome our obstacles? The human brain is designed to create a story. We learn the story model by beginning, middle, and end concepts.

See? Those characters that we grow to love are made from the essence of being human, and that is why we begin to love them—because they show us humanity. Those characters come from the paths we have walked, from the mountains we have climbed, and the lakes we have swum across. Our humanness gives us direct access to compassion, love, and respect, and the only reason we ever get away from it is that we develop the habit.

Psychologist Kristin Neff was the first person to measure and operationally define the term *self-compassion.* She defines *self-compassion* as kindness toward the self, which entails being gentle, supportive, and understanding. "Rather than harshly judging oneself for personal shortcomings, the self is offered warmth and unconditional acceptance." Wow, kindness toward self sounds like a foreign process to some of us, especially once we hear it for the first time. I believe, at this point with everything that we have learned we are not only practicing self-compassion but we are open to it — aren't we?

As kids, we heard messages like "Be kind to others." Yes, it's still noble. Still, it sounds like the messaging should be, "Present kindness toward self and others and have healthy boundaries with those who cannot respect your compassionate lifestyle." Yes, it's quite a mouthful to say to a child, but can we afford to be lazy?

I don't think we can afford that outdated mindset any

further. We owe it to one another and the betterment of the next generation to teach them self-compassion. We owe it to ourselves to recognize that the truth about our story is that there is light, there is love, there is a beacon of freedom that we currently have access to. For us, we don't have to search; we don't have to change. All we have to do is become totally present and recognize how much love is available to us, even if it's a little—that is more than enough.

You can always treat yourself well and talk kindly to yourself. And on those days when you are deep in the unruliest feelings, recognize that you have the strength to meet it. Please honor the fact that you always have access to self-compassion.

We no longer run from any emotion, conversation, or thought. We now learn to observe and to hold it fully, no matter how dark, light, deep, weak, shallow, or strong. Self-compassion is about tapping into the depths of each moment. We recognize now that self-compassion is about allowing yourself to authentically process what you are going through—that is freedom.

The shame, guilt, and judgment that come with some of the darker emotions no longer have power in our bodies because we don't run from those emotions; we recognize that we have power and that it's okay to honor, acknowledge, and use the material of these emotional states to propel us. We make space for them, we see them, we allow ourselves to be immersed in shame if that is what is happening. If we are deeply ashamed, that's okay because, at that moment, we are living in our deepest humanity — we are allowed to drive that space, to ask for a community to witness us and we are allowed to process what we are feeling. We now make space to reflect on our story with a compassionate inner voice, no matter how hard it is. We are at a point where we can face all sides of the human experience.

We must allow ourselves to stop and experience the joys of song, the rhythm of dance, and the fire of our soul as it burns fully into this majestic life. We are beautiful, and what makes us this way is our fullness, our depth, and everything about our story. Hopefully through our practices here, we are at a point where our psyche feels engaged into our world, where we follow our callings—whatever that may be in that moment.

Living Fully With Thankfulness

As we begin to inquire deeply into our lives, we will recognize that there is so much to be thankful for, there is so much to honor and to smile about, there is so much in our lives that is worthy of acknowledgment.

I noticed one of the deepest shifts in my day-to-day moods when I started embracing thankfulness as a way of life. I have a story for you that embodies this.

For the second time in an six-year period, my bike was stolen from a community bike lock area; and this time, it was in a gated community where key fobs were needed to access the space, and there were cameras. When I went to the bike room to grab my bike for an afternoon ride, I was so naive, and I didn't assume that my bike was stolen as I looked at bike pad no. 38 with a blank stare.

The funny thing about it was, just like the first time my bike was stolen about six years ago, the chain that I purchased was in the place that I left it, but the bike wasn't. Ha! I walked down to the leasing office to see what the agent had to say. I didn't care for her demeanor at all; she was instantly defensive and had no empathy or compassion for the situation. It was like she was ready to go to war for whatever her company told her and she wasn't ready to be empathetic to the realization that the bike was stolen. I said, "Good morning. My bike was in no. 38, and I'm ready to retrieve it."

She said, "Okay, I can give you the police report, and you have to go through insurance."

I said, "Huh? What do you mean?"

She said, "Well, we had a break-in." I'll be honest. At that moment, I was triggered, I was angry, I was deep into the depths of that shocking revelation. Attempting to process what she was saying plus her lack of empathy, and her sub-zero face sent me into a downward spiral of emotion. I just walked away. I went back to the house and asked Daisy if she could handle it for me. I knew I didn't have the capacity to bring any love or calmness to that situation. I offered myself self-compassion and let it go. I knew I needed help to handle that situation especially since it instantly triggered me. I needed to get to my appointment so asking for help, breathing into my body and letting it go at that moment was my best choice.

The next day, when I got on the phone with my therapist, he asked me, "What's coming up for you today, Sylvester?" And what I felt was a deep sense of gratitude, a deep appreciation for life, a love for life. I was able to recognize that I could buy hundreds and maybe even thousands of bikes if I wanted to. I recognized that my bike being stolen was not the end of my world; in fact, it really didn't matter at all.

At first, yes, I had an initial inner reaction, but I met it, I heard it, and I let it go. Twenty-four hours later, I was totally unconcerned with the loss. Just to be pragmatic, yes, I must say that I do not want to buy a new bike every single day. And of course, I want the next one to not be stolen; but even if it is, does it matter?

I was able to recognize that everything is going well in my life, and when it's not, I am going to honor and meet the hardship, I'll process the emotions, I'll find a way to work on my inner voice, and I'll try my best to treat myself with self-compassion. I connected with a layer of consciousness that was laced in thankfulness for the fruits of life, for the blessings that I've been given and earned, and for the community of people that I have access to.

At that moment in my life, I was holding on to a strong desire to get this book right, to finish it strong, to be a great father, to be a great friend, and all my desires were creating an immense emotional pressure. The bike being stolen forced me to let go of the identity I had as a bike owner, it forced me to recognize the stress and pressure that I was carrying and it made me consider a change. It forced me to recognize that things change, and that's okay. The bike was a symbol that triggered me to realize I needed to let go.

My naivety showed me that I don't assume that bad things will happen to me, and it showed me that it's okay to be human, to have loss, to have anger, to have thankfulness, to have love, to have the full gamut of the human experience flow through my psyche, body, and mind. That moment showed me that thankfulness, gratitude, the ability to recognize opportunity, and love are a blessing. It was a time where I felt like I went totally home to my body, to my mind, to my psyche with nothing but love and honor. And in the following days, weeks, and months, I was able to repeat it and stay in that groove.

I hope from the bottom of my heart that the stories, poetry, bullet points, ideas, and words here deeply invite you into your home—into you. I hope that you are able to love yourself properly every single day for the rest of your life. I hope that you are able to find thankfulness in this very moment. I hope you are able to recognize the growth that you've made, the effort that you've put forth, and just how much power is inside you. I am a strong believer that we will always be given what we need when we ask. I believe that if you want to be held, you must open your hands, and you must be willing to hold another.

I hope this book held a safe space for you. I hope these words were able to trigger a movement in your psyche. In *Loving Yourself Properly*, you read the words *us*, *we*, and *love* at least 150 times each. I told you on the first page that we could accept this invitation together. My friend, we did it; we took the invitation to love ourselves properly. With love, with everything I have to offer, thank you. I am so thankful that we could go on this journey together. I appreciate you for giving this book a chance. I am so grateful and thankful that you read this entire book and I hope to keep serving you in the future. From the bottom of my heart and through all of the energy that is running through me today, all I can say to you is Thank you! Thank you for giving me a chance to share my words with you. I am so grateful for the opportunity to serve you through this book and I'm deeply honored for the space we cultivated here. I hope you see, create, and cherish all the love that is in your life.

with love,

Sylvester McNutt III

Acknowledgments

I'm so grateful for everyone who has been in my life, especially most recently. This is the first book that I have released where I can say that I am a father. The experience of being a parent has brought such an immense richness and depth to my life. I'm finding new ways to love myself and those around me, and for that, I am overwhelmed with gratitude.

I am grateful for Daisy and her contributions to our son's life. You model what it means to be a great mother, and I'm thankful for the opportunity to assist you in your journey as a mother.

Mason, my son, is an energetic soul, and it's been an honor to watch him grow from a seed to what he is today. Mason, if you ever see these words, son, please be kind and gentle to yourself. Keep eating your fruits, vegetables, and keep moving around. Also, you love sleep. If you can continue to cherish your sleep patterns, I promise, it will only support you son.

I want to offer myself some compassion because this was my most challenging book to write. The transition of becoming a parent, writing during the 2020 pandemic, and moving brought many changes and challenges. I'm glad that I found some self-compassion and further healing throughout this journey.

I'm so thankful for my friends, family, and haters, too, ha! And lastly, I want to acknowledge you for making the sharing of this journey possible. I'm so thankful for your presence as a friend, as a reader, and someone who is curious about this conversation. Without you, I wouldn't exist (as an author, ha). With love, see you soon!

NOTES

Bedrick, David. "Understanding Shame: Symptoms and Prevention." *Psychology Today* (Sept. 14, 2016). www.psychologytoday.com/us/blog/is-psychology-making-us-sick/201609/understanding-shame-symptoms-and-prevention.

Davis, Vauna. "Recognizing the Red Flags of Shame." *Reach 10*, 2017. https://reach10.Org/Recognizing-Red-Flags-Shame/.

Firestone, Tamsen. "How Your Critical Inner Voice Gets in the Way of Love." *PsychAlive*, May 29, 2018. https://www.psychalive.org/critical-inner-voice-gets-in-the-way-of-love/.

Frothingham, Scott. "How Long Does It Take for a New Behavior to Become Automatic?" Edited by Timothy J. Legg, PhD, CRNP. *The World Counts*, Oct. 24, 2019. https://www.theworldcounts.com/happiness/psychology-of-habits.

Chowdhury, Madhuleena Roy. "The Science and Psychology of Goal-Setting 101." PositivePsychology.com, Sept. 1, 2020. https://positivepsychology.com/goal-setting-psychology/.

Duhigg, Charles. "The Power of Habit." *Experience Life*, July 15, 2020. https://experiencelife.com/ article/the-power-of-habit/.

Johnson, Lorie. "Power of Habit: The Key to Breaking Harmful Patterns." CBN News, Jan. 2 2015. https://www1.cbn.com/cbnnews/healthscience/2013/april/power-of-habit-the-key-to-breaking-harmful-patterns/.

"Michael Scofield." Prison Break Wiki. https://prisonbreak.fandom.com/wiki/Michael_Scofield.

Weller, Francis. "Healing Shame." https://www.francisweller.net/store/p2/Healing_Shame%3A_ Caring_for_the_Wounded_Heart.html.

World Counts, The. "Psychology of Habits," 2020. https://www.theworldcounts.com/happiness/psychology-of-habits.

Loving Yourself Properly

The End

Printed in Great Britain
by Amazon

25295500R00205